# Tales of Old Texas

## or

# The Adventures of Bullfrog

## Weldon Reed

ISBN 978-1-64349-671-9 (paperback)
ISBN 978-1-64349-672-6 (digital)

Christian Faith Publishing, Inc.
832 Park Avenue
Meadville, PA 16335
www.christianfaithpublishing.com

Printed in the United States of America

# CONTENTS

# INTRODUCTION

Just call me Bullfrog. That's not really my name, but it was my nickname when I was little, growing up in Cleburne, Texas, in the 1940s and 1950s. My Uncle O. B., who had a junkyard on the corner of Boone St. and Sabine St. on the northeast side of town, gave me the name. I'm not sure why he chose that particular nickname. Perhaps it was because I had a big mouth and a long tongue like a frog. After all, how many people do you know who can touch the end of their nose with the tip of their tongue? It looks rather unsightly, so I don't usually demonstrate that ability in public. However, it could be that my uncle nicknamed me Bullfrog because my mentality was on par with a frog. Now that is probably closer to the truth especially when it came to gullibility and doing stupid things.

This book is dedicated to my supportive wife Freida and to my long-suffering children--Cindy, Tim, Laura, Jim, Ryan, Karen, and Laurie--who had to listen to these stories via the oral tradition but now can read them in printed form. I would add special thanks to daughter Laurie for her yeoman labor on this book in arranging and typing all the chapter titles plus correcting or undoing all of my computer errors.

Weldon

# CHAPTER 1

## EATING ROOSTER'S EGGS

I would believe anything my Uncle O. B. told me. When I was about eight, he told me that if I were to eat a rooster's eggs, I could fly like a rooster. Now at the time, we raised chickens, but I told my uncle that I did not think our Rhode Island Red rooster laid eggs. He said, "When you gathered eggs, didn't you see some with speckles on 'em?"

I replied, "Yeah."

"Well, those were the rooster's eggs. Have your mother fry two or three of those without the all-white or all-brown ones mixed in, and you'll be able to fly!"

What eight-year-old would turn down a chance like that—to fly over the neighborhood like Superman? The next morning, my dad did not even have to tell me to go get the eggs. I was up at sunrise, knocking the hens off their nests and looking for speckled eggs. Sure enough, I found three, ran into the house, handed them to Mom, and asked her to fry them for me. Fortunately, she did not ask me why but was just tickled that I was that hungry.

After eating them, I waited for hours for the feathers to sprout on my arms, but they didn't appear. I mournfully trudged up the street to Uncle O. B.'s junkyard, where he was cutting up an old car, and told him it didn't work. He asked, "What didn't work?" (He had forgotten what he told me the day before.)

"Eating rooster's eggs," I glumly replied. "Feathers aren't growing at all."

"Oh," he said. "I didn't say feathers would grow. You just need to flap your arms real hard and fast, and up you'll go!"

I immediately began flapping my arms like mad, just about dislocating my shoulders, but nothing happened.

Uncle O. B. said, "Oh, I see the problem. You need some height. You need to climb up on something and jump, flapping your arms, and off you will go."

To this day, I shudder thinking about that because Uncle O. B.'s junkyard and house on Sabine was just one block away from the overpass over the Santa Fe railroad track on Boone Street (about seventy feet high). Fortunately for me, instead of heading to the overpass, I ran to my house three houses away and eagerly climbed up on our front porch. There I stood on the edge of the porch roof, thinking of the impression I would make on all of my friends as I came soaring over the treetops. Well, after I jumped, I made an impression all right—a belly buster from ten feet high. After hearing my screams, my mother came running out the front door; and after I sobbed to her what I had done and why, she called my uncle on the phone.

Trust me—with Mom being a redhead—she gave him a piece of her mind, and then some.

# CHAPTER 2

# THE COTTON PATCH

Did you know that a cotton stalk has other uses besides just bearing cotton? When I was six years old, my dad decided to introduce me to the cotton patch. On a Saturday, I was to accompany him to a cotton field near Covington for my first experience (but by no means my last) at picking cotton. Especially for the occasion, my mother sewed me a little cotton sack with shoulder strap; it was about three feet long.

As Dad drove into the field and parked, he pointed out to me all this white stuff growing on these plants. All I had to do was pick the cotton off the stalk and put it into my sack. When I had filled my sack, I was to drag it over to this wooden wagon with high walls, where a man there would hoist it up and hang it on these scales to weigh it. He would then keep a record of the weight of the cotton that I picked, and I would receive five dollars for every one hundred pounds that I gathered. Now Daddy told me that he would keep half of what I earned to help buy my clothes, but I could spend the other half on however I wanted. Boy, I was getting excited. Visions of dollar signs danced in my head. I was going to get rich. I was going to buy a Roy Rogers twin cap pistol set, maybe a new bike, maybe even a Red Ryder BB gun!

Enthusiastically, I started down this row of cotton, my fingers just flying as I plucked the cotton and eagerly thrust it into my sack. I just knew by the end of the day my pockets would be bulging with dollar bills. Now these rows were about seventy-five yards long; I finished that first one and started back on another one. I did feel a little tiredness coming on, but I didn't care, for riches awaited me! When I finished that second row, my little sack looked like it could be getting full, so I dragged it over to the wagon for the man to weigh it—two pounds! Oh, man! Getting rich was going to be harder than I thought!

With my enthusiasm waning, I trudged over to a new row and disconsolately began my now weary task of picking that cotton. I admit I was getting pretty glum about the prospect of obtaining wealth. Just then, my foot kicked a tennis ball-sized rock that was lying on the ground between the rows of cotton. Wait a minute! I now knew how I could speed up this weighing process! So as I worked my way down that cotton row, I started alternating—a handful of cotton, one rock; more cotton, another rock. When I finished a second row using my new method, my sack was now feeling fairly heavy. Tickled pink with my witty scheme, I lugged my sack over to the wagon again, where the man dutifully weighed it for me. Aha! Nine pounds! Now you're talking! The dollar signs were once more bouncing around in my head.

The gentleman offered to empty my sack into the wagon for me, but I instantly knew that would not be good. Remember that this was a wooden wagon, which also meant a wooden floor. I did not want him to hear the *klunk-klunk* as some of the rocks in my sack hit that bottom, so I cheerfully thanked him but said I could handle it. I would just climb up on the side of the wagon and dump the sack. I made sure, though, to walk around to the far side of the wagon from where the man stood by the scales, and I planned on gently pouring the cotton/rocks out.

As I reached the other side of the wagon, I thought my scheme was working perfectly. Unfortunately, just then, my dad came around the back of the wagon with his full sack that resembled a dragon's neck; it was that big and full. He grabbed my sack and said he would dump it for me, which he did. Yes, there were a good number of *klunk-klunks* heard. Then Daddy introduced me to another usage of a cotton stalk besides just bearing cotton.

# CHAPTER 3

# "ME DONKEY AND ME"

If you remember that Harry Belafonte song, "Hold 'Em Joe," then that means you are just about as old as I am. Now the particular donkey I have in mind did not really belong to me, but we did share a close relationship upon one occasion. The donkey belonged to my uncle, Ed Reed, from Bossier City, Louisiana. Uncle Ed and his son James had come to visit my Uncle O. B. (you remember him, the one who told me about the rooster's eggs), who lived on the corner of

Sabine Street and Boone Street and ran a junkyard behind his house. Since we lived just four houses down from Uncle O. B., my daddy, my brother Eldon, and I were up at my uncle's house visiting with Uncle Ed and James.

While in town, Uncle Ed had visited the farmer's market a couple of blocks south of the courthouse and had purchased a donkey. The gentleman from whom he had bought it would not deliver it to Bossier City, naturally, but he delivered it instead to Uncle O. B.'s house. While we were all standing around in Uncle O. B.'s front yard looking at the donkey, my Uncle O. B. had a brilliant idea and asked, "Do you boys want to ride him?" Without waiting for an answer, he grabbed my cousin James, who was two years older than I and the same age as my brother Eldon, and swung him up on the donkey's back. He told James, who was about nine, to hold onto the reins. Then my uncle picked up my brother and placed him on the donkey behind James. He turned to me and queried, "Bullfrog, do you want to ride him too?" Again, not even giving me a choice (I was just about to say no), Uncle O. B. grabbed me and set me behind my brother.

Now picture this scene, if you will. Where am I sitting? What room is left on this ordinary-sized donkey? That is correct. I am sitting on the donkey's derriere. Next question: what do I hold on to? I suppose I could grab the tail, but what would that accomplish? Thus, I did the only thing I could do; I got a death grip on my brother. Then James kicked the donkey in the ribs to get it trotting down the graveled street, but it didn't budge. Now my Uncle O. B., the one with the great ideas, picked up a strand of "bobwire" (okay, I know it's spelled "barbed wire," but that is how we pronounced in those days) and proceeded to double it over and whacked the inert donkey across that same derriere just below where I was sitting. Hey, that certainly got its attention, and he lunged out of Uncle O. B.'s yard as if his tail were on fire, with me holding on for dear life. By its third or fourth gallop, I was leaning hard a port and screaming bloody murder. Eldon was yelling too but for me to turn him loose.

Looking back, I now certainly wish I *had* turned him loose for when I fell and hit the gravel like a ton of bricks, I had pulled Eldon right down on top of me. Lucky me, he landed on my left arm, and I heard a distinct snap. Excruciating pain immediately shot through my arm, and I jumped to my feet crying, bawling, if you will. All of the men were laughing their heads off, thinking my plight was hilarious.

Now I wanted consoling and care, not laughter, so I took off running for home and to Mother's arms. She could hear me crying and ran out our front door to see what was going on. She hugged me as I ran up to her, yelling about my hurt arm. She took one look and saw the jagged white bone tip protruding through the skin of my elbow. Then she marched me back up the street to Uncle O. B.'s house, where the men were still laughing. I believe I forgot to mention that my mother was redheaded, and she was good and mad about her baby boy being hurt by the carelessness or foolishness of my uncles and her husband. Don't ask me why, but even today, when I spot a donkey in a pasture, I look with fondness at it and not aversion. I can't help it; I'm an avowed animal lover.

# CHAPTER 4

## YOUNG LOVE

Some kids arrive late to the romance scene—some start early. I was one of the early ones. Cupid drilled me with one of his arrows when I was in the second grade. Ruby was her name, but I was much too bashful to openly confess my undying love for her. However, I devised another way to reveal my devotion. I would write a love note and put it on her shelf in the cloakroom above where she hung her coat.

Therefore, after working on the note the night before, I hurriedly walked to Santa Fe Elementary the next morning, slipped into our cloakroom, and surreptitiously placed the missive on her shelf. I then walked down the aisle to my seat and anxiously awaited Ruby's arrival. Sure enough, a few minutes later, she arrived and disappeared into the cloakroom. My little heart was all atwitter, anticipating her coming out of the cloakroom, smiling and blushing. Well, she came out all right, but there was a stern frown on her face; and instead of her making her way to her seat a few desks up from mine, she did a right turn and marched up to Ms. Spell's desk. I could not make out what she said to our teacher, but I did hear my name being mentioned. Ms. Spell then said, "Weldon, would you come up here please?"

With a certain amount of trepidation, I slowly walked to her desk and said, "Yes, Ma'am?"

"Ruby found this love note in her locker, and though it wasn't signed, she thinks you wrote it."

I innocently asked, "May I see it?" She politely handed it to me. I looked at it, and then stated, "Ms. Spell, that is not my handwriting!"

Ms. Spell took another look at it and agreed with me, saying, "Ruby, Weldon is right. That is not his handwriting. Weldon, you may go to your seat." I smugly sat back down, knowing that I had deviously fooled the unsuspecting again. (My older sister Melba had written the note for me.)

I don't remember much about Cupid being around in third or fourth grade, but he did strike in fifth grade. A new girl had started attending Santa Fe, and her name was Mary, a beautiful brunette. To me, she was prettier than Tom Sawyer's Becky Thatcher. Naturally, my love for her was strictly platonic. I worshipped her from afar the entire school year for she was much too attractive for me to even attempt to engage in conversation. So I would watch her from a distance and sigh wistfully, knowing little freckled-faced me had no chance to ever walk with her and certainly never hold hands. After fifth grade ended and summer arrived, a friend of mine told me that Mary was transferring to Irving Elementary.

Right then and there, I determined I was going to transfer too, to follow the love of my life. For some reason, the details of arranging this sort of slipped my mind. All I know is, sure enough, my mother enrolled me in Irving for sixth grade. I was on cloud nine. I was going to be close to Mary again, and hopefully this time, I would get up enough nerve to actually talk to her and maybe profess my undying devotion to her. Unfortunately, that idea did not last long because Mary took up with the best-looking (and biggest) guy in sixth grade. My poor heart was shattered, to say the least.

Now I had told this romantic story for years during my adult life until one time, at a family gathering, I happened to repeat this sad story of unrequited love, and my sister and mother stopped me. Mother said, "Weldon, what a preposterous story! You don't remember Mr. Cook, the vice principal of Santa Fe, coming to our house that summer after fifth grade and asking me if I would transfer you to Irving because Santa Fe needed a rest from you?"

What romantic young lad would want to remember such a harsh reality as that?

# Chapter 5

## The Popsicle and the Grasshopper

Years ago, when I was about twelve, I was walking home down Sabine Street, returning from Fletcher's grocery. I was licking on my favorite Popsicle, a double-stick raspberry one. Sabine Street was graveled at that time, and if you wanted to avoid getting run over by cars or being showered by gravel, you had to walk on the dirt sidewalk parallel to the street, alongside the fences where various neighbors had cows, horses, or chickens.

As I walked along the dirt path enjoying my Popsicle, I noticed someone approaching me on the same path—Offie. Offie was a neighborhood boy, a year or two younger than I but one tough customer. His real name was Arthur, but no one dared call him that—he preferred Offie. He had an older brother named Wolfie, another nickname naturally, but we kids on the street did not know his real name and had better sense than to inquire. He was even meaner than Offie.

So Offie was walking toward me and saw my Popsicle. His eyes lit up, and he began to smile. Now I knew that I had lost this Popsicle. I could fight him for it, but he and I had tangled a couple of weeks earlier over who was the toughest. After he had bloodied my nose, puffed my lips, and loosened my teeth, I had reluctantly accepted his higher ranking in the pecking order in the neighborhood. Another choice would be to try to outrun him, which I probably could, but he would just jump me later and make me regret that idea.

However, I did not want to just *hand* it over to him like a chicken, so I attempted something rather feeble—I licked all over the Popsicle, front and back, top to bottom. (Well, it always worked with girls!) Offie just smiled even more broadly and suddenly snatched a grasshopper that was sitting on top of one of the cedar posts holding up the adjacent fence. Without hesitation, he calmly bit the grasshopper's head off and spat it on the ground.

I handed him my Popsicle.

# CHAPTER 6

# DADDY AND THE BEEHIVE

W hen I was about ten years old, my family was visiting my Uncle Doc and Aunt Alice, who lived near Kilgore. Uncle Doc had a beehive sitting on the bank of a small tank near his house. From time to time, he would gather the honey. Unfortunately, while he was doing so about two weeks before, he had gotten stung several times and had a severe reaction to the stings, winding up in the hospital. While we were there, just sitting around and talking, Uncle Doc happened to mention to Daddy that the honey needed to be gathered, but Uncle Doc was a little apprehensive about doing so.

Naturally, Daddy said he would be glad to do, so he donned the hat with the netting covering it, and off he went. He was also wearing a long-sleeved shirt with the sleeves buttoned and was wearing cotton gloves to protect his hands. My cousin Mousey (his real name was James, and we were the same age) suggested he and I should follow along and watch, but we were going to do it from the water. Uncle Doc had welded two old Buick hoods together to form a makeshift boat. It was rather tricky sitting in it, but we had two-gallon cans for seats and two small boards for paddles. We paddled over near Daddy and the beehive, about ten feet away from the excitement.

To Mousey's dying day, he swore that I popped off and said something to Daddy about "Hope you get stung," but I knew better than to do that for I knew my daddy would do something in retaliation. As Daddy was nonchalantly putting hunks of honeycomb into a bucket, he suddenly turned and underhanded one piece, which was covered with bees, into the boat between Mousey and me. I froze stiff, really shocked that Daddy would actually do something like that to his own son! However, Mousey chose action, and he dove over the side of the boat into the water. He lit out for shore, half swimming and half running. He came the closest to walking on water since the Apostle Peter!

Fortunately for me, the bees were attracted by all of Mousey's movements and chased him, not even bothering me. To me, that was appropriate because I knew it was he who opened his big mouth and yelled that he hoped Daddy would get stung. My freezing in place was one of the few smart things I did when I was that age.

# CHAPTER 7

# A JAILBIRD AT AGE TWELVE

Would you believe I got arrested when I was twelve years old? I was on my bike, pedaling down Sabine Street to Fletcher's store as I frequently did, when suddenly, I was flung over the handlebars. I landed on my hands, chest, and knees, skinning them up pretty badly. I slowly got to my feet and set my bike upright to try to find out what happened. That's when I discovered that my front wheel would not turn, so I glumly dragged the bike back home to take the wheel apart.

After dismantling the wheel, I discovered that one of the wheel bearings was not turning at all. Several of its ball bearings were fused solid. There was a serial number on the bearing, so I told Mom I was going to walk downtown to the Western Auto store on East Henderson to buy a new one. After trudging the three miles to downtown, I walked into the store, went straight to the bicycle section, and started hunting for the right wheel bearing. I located the ones with the right serial number and saw the price was thirty-five cents.

Now I had about a dollar and a half in my pocket, having visited my money sock in my drawer before I left home. However, I did not see any sense in just throwing money away, so after carefully looking around and not seeing anyone glancing my way, I surreptitiously slipped the wheel bearing into my front pocket and casually strolled to the front door. As I opened it and started to step outside, a large hand suddenly grabbed my shoulder, and a man's voice said, "Get back in here, kid." This man dragged me over the counter, and then he called the police. Sitting me down in a chair, he said we would wait for the police to show up.

About ten minutes later, a police car pulled up in the back alley; and surely, the largest policeman in Cleburne walked through the door. He was as big as Goliath, it seemed like. He took a death grip on my wrist, dragged me out to the car, and put me in the back seat behind the wire mesh separating the front seat from the back seat. He drove the three blocks down to the police station and led me inside where he took me down this hallway and sat me down in a cell. He then closed the door and walked off.

Looking back many years from then, I could see that the policeman doing all of this was probably scare tactics on his part, and they were partly working, but I was a brazen little rascal and put up as brave a front as I could. I sat in that cell for about thirty minutes when Goliath showed up again, unlocked the door, and grabbing my wrist, dragged me outside and up the two blocks to the courthouse. I was just hoping I had the chance to pull away from him because I figured I could outrun him, but he was just about squeezing blood out of my hand. We went up to the third floor to the juvenile officer's office. Now this man really read me the riot act! You would have sworn that I had broken into Fort Knox or something instead of pilfering a measly thirty-five-cent wheel bearing. Then he started the third degree on me.

"What's your name, son?"

Naturally, I lied and gave him some fictitious name.

"Where do you live?" he asked.

"I come from Illinois, and I'm just here visiting my aunt and uncle," I replied.

"What's their names?"

I told him that I did not remember since I didn't know them that well, but if he would let me go, I was sure I could find their house. Unfortunately, he wasn't buying that, but then he asked me if I remembered anything about their house or neighborhood. At that moment, an idea started forming in my mind; I might be able to get out of this mess unscathed. I told him that I did remember an overpass over some railroad tracks. He stated that he knew where that was, so grabbing my wrist like Goliath had done, he marched me downstairs and to his car.

Not being successful at escaping from the policeman, I was hoping to have a better chance getting away from this older man. My first idea was when he would put me in his car. If he sat me in the passenger side and walked around to the driver's side, I would fly out my door and be gone, for I knew all of the alleys and backstreets of Cleburne. However, the juvenile officer had probably had this pulled on him before because instead, he led me around to the driver's side and slid me under the steering wheel and thus over to the passenger side. (Drat it!)

Now as we were driving over to Boone Street and the overpass over the Santa Fe tracks, sheer genius hit me! I knew who my aunt and uncle were going to be. Three houses north of our house on Sabine lived an elderly couple. The old man was as deaf as a doorknob, and his pocket hearing aid rarely worked. In addition, his wife was as blind as a bat and wore the original Coke bottle glasses. The officer, in order to communicate with either one, would definitely have to turn loose of my hand. The instant he did, I would zip around to the back of the couple's house and through the fence into the Santa Fe shops, which was my playground.

Boy, I felt so relieved that I had it all worked out. We drove over the overpass and dropped down to Sabine, turning the corner there and passing my real uncle's house, Uncle O. B. and his junk-yard. I sort of scrunched down in the seat so Aunt Violet or any of my cousins would not see me. Two empty lots down sat the old couple's house on the right. I excitedly told the juvenile officer that was my aunt and uncle's house. Again, I briefly had the thought that he might get out on his side and walk around to me, giving me the opportunity to fly out my door and disappear. However, no such luck. He merely pulled me underneath the steering wheel again and out on his side.

Okay, I was still going to get out of this. If the old man opened the door, the juvenile officer was going to have to turn loose of my hand, and I'm gone. If his wife opened the door, he could not com-municate with her either without dropping my hand, and I'm gone then too. Therefore, I confidently walked beside the officer and waited as he knocked on the door. It opened, and there stood my mother, visiting the elderly couple.

I have repressed from my memory what followed.

# CHAPTER 8

## SMOKE, SMOKE, SMOKE
## THAT CIGARETTE

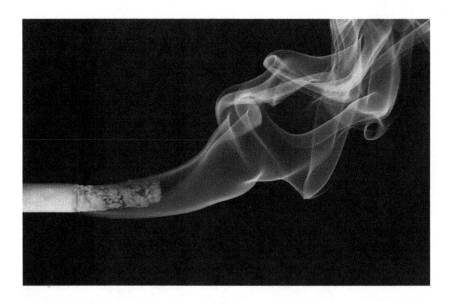

When I was around twelve or thirteen, most of the boys my age in my neighborhood of northeast Cleburne smoked to some degree. Most of us had corncob pipes ala Tom Sawyer and Huck Finn, which of course, we kept hidden from our parents especially our mothers. We also usually had a red can of Prince Albert pipe tobacco that we had either purchased at the neighborhood store or "borrowed" from across the counter while the owner wasn't looking.

Even at Santa Fe Elementary School in the fourth and fifth grades, we would sneak off campus at recess and walk two blocks down to the little store. There, we would buy a Flor de Melba for a nickel or a King Edward for a dime and puff furiously on them as we walked back to the school. We never could finish them, so we would extinguish them and hide them in nearby bushes and pick them up after school.

On one particular summer afternoon, I was with two buddies of mine, Ronnie and Carol, roaming through the Santa Fe shops behind my house on Sabine, exploring old railroad cars and cabooses. I had not taken time when I left my house to grab my pipe, which I kept hidden in our storage shed out back, so I asked the other two if they had brought theirs. They hadn't either. Ronnie suggested that we could walk the five blocks down to the store and buy a pack of cigarettes or snatch a pack while one of us distracted the owner.

However, I said, "Wait a minute. I know where my dad keeps his cigarettes under the bed. I'll slip into Mom and Dad's bedroom and swipe a pack." The other guys thought that was a swell idea, so off I scooted home. Arriving at the house, I quietly slipped in our back door, which opened right in my parents' bedroom. I could hear Mom banging some pots and pans in the kitchen, so the coast was clear for me to grab a pack. I knelt down at the head of Dad's bed, and, sure enough, there were his cigarettes on the floor back against the wall. There was one slight problem, though. What I had found was a brand-new carton of Luckies, unopened.

Now common sense would have told anyone to just open the carton and take out only one pack. However, my little beady brain rarely ever looked that far ahead. I usually just acted on the impulse of the moment, and my impulse told me, "Eureka! I had just struck it rich!" Thus, I grabbed the whole carton and ducked out the back door. When I got back to the boxcar where Ronnie and Carol were waiting, they could not believe our good fortune—ten packs of Luckies! Man, we were in paradise—two hundred cigarettes! I had taken the time to grab a box of matches from my stash in the storage shed, and we commenced to smoke, and smoke, and smoke. We would smoke three cigarettes at a time, placing them between each of our fingers on our left hands.

Smoke was just about billowing out the door of that deserted boxcar that we were sitting in. We would only smoke them about halfway down and then just toss them out the door on the gravel ballast there beside the railroad track. Would you believe we smoked that entire carton in about two and a half hours? Sick? I imagine! My face was so white that you could count every freckle on it—and I had a bunch then! Ronnie and Carol were in the same shape but, man, what an accomplishment!

We climbed out of the boxcar and staggered over to the wooden fence that separated the Santa Fe shops property from the residences along Sabine Street. We then crawled through it, swinging one of the boards aside, and separated to go to our respective homes.

As my luck would have it, Daddy was home from working at Bell Helicopter in Saginaw, and as my worse luck would have it, he was out of cigarettes. Naturally, when he attempted to retrieve his new carton, he found it missing—imagine that! He did not even bother to ask my sister Melba or my older brother Eldon what had happened to his cigarettes.

I heard him bellowing, "Weldon Thomas," as I came in the back door. I think my breath even knocked *him* over. If my memory serves me correctly, the dreaded black belt (actually a razor strap used for sharpening straightedge razors) came out of Daddy's closet. However, he clearly did not beat me to death then, for I am still here.

# CHAPTER 9

## MOSE AND THE SNAKE

When I was growing up in Cleburne, our next-door neighbor was named Mose, and he loved to go fishing with Daddy and me. The time I remember involved our not fishing with poles or trotline but instead, "grabbling." Now for those who don't know, "grabbling" is catching fish with your bare hands after you have found them underneath big rocks in a river or in holes under the river bank. (Oklahomans call it "noodling." Texans call it "grabbling.")

Mose did not get in the water and grabble with us; he was a mite too spooky for that. You could poke your finger at him suddenly, and he would jump two feet backward. So when he went with us, he would walk along the bank carrying a tow sack, and when Dad or I caught a fish, we would toss it up to Mose to put in the sack. Now what really tickled Mose was for him to hold the tow sack open and catch the fish on the fly, like a Willie Mays basket catch.

Well, one time when we were out engaging in this slightly illegal sport, Dad and I were feeling around underneath this big rock in the Brazos River near Whitney. We were in water that came to my chest (I was about thirteen or fourteen at the time), but the water was only thigh deep to Dad. I had to hold my breath, close my eyes, and dive down in the brown water to feel around. When I came up about the second time, Dad had a grin on his face from ear to ear. "There's a snake on my side," he whispered since we were only about five yards off the bank. I immediately commenced looking for *another* rock since that one had just lost its appeal.

My philosophy in grabbling was that if I did not instantly feel large scales or fins on whatever live object I touched under a rock or in a hole, I left that area in a hurry. However, my dad did not share that same feeling as, unfortunately, Mose discovered.

"Hey, Mose!" Dad yelled.

"Yeah, Jay!" Mose answered.

"I've got a big 'un under here," Dad replied.

"Fine, Jay! Toss him here!" Mose responded, excitedly holding the tow sack open.

I saw Dad's shoulder drop down as he reached under the rock, and then he quickly rose up out of the water with that writhing water moccasin in his hand, and in the same motion, cartwheeled it through the air at Mose! I've never seen such terror on a man's face in all my life. Poor Mose broke all existing speed records at going backward, and over an obstacle course too, what with those bushes and small trees he flattened in the process. Of course, Daddy and I nearly drowned while laughing our heads off.

It was some time before Mose went fishing with us again. Imagine that.

# CHAPTER 10

# MORE GRABBLIN' STORIES

Poking your hands underneath rocks or in holes along a riverbank feeling for fish is not for everybody, but my dad did so with no trepidation whatsoever.

On one occasion when Dad went grabbling without me, he and some friends of his brought a seine and stretched it along the bank of this tributary of the Brazos River near Whitney. Dad and another man got inside the seine while two others held the ends up against the bank, and two others stayed outside the seine, standing on the bottom of the seine to be sure no fish escaped underneath it. Dad began thrusting his foot into holes underneath the bank to see if he could spook any fish to dart out and into the net, where the men outside the seine could wrap them up and carry the fish up on the bank.

At the time, Dad was wearing an unlaced pair of old Army boots. Just as he stuck his foot into one particular hole, something grabbed it and began shaking it like a dog would a snake. Naturally, he jerked his foot back, but whatever had a hold of his foot was biting down so hard that Dad's boot came off. Now what did my dad do? Did he leave the premises immediately like any sane person would've—and especially me? Not at all! He merely lifted the other boot out of the water, tied its laces, and then stuck *that* foot back in the hole.

Quicker than a cat can blink, whatever was in there grabbed that boot too and began shaking it back and forth. Real easy like, Dad slid his foot out and seized what was biting his foot—a big catfish! Dad and his friends weighed it later, and it tipped the scales at twenty-eight pounds. At the time, our local sporting goods store in Cleburne held a weekly fishing contest for the largest fish caught. Since Dad didn't catch his in a quite "legal" manner, he proceeded to hook that catfish on a trotline and entered it in the contest. Would you believe he won a ball of trotline cord about the size of a basketball? That's my dad, all right.

It wasn't that we couldn't catch fish the legal ways, because we could, but grabbling or seining was just more exciting and adventuresome. One time, we were grabbling with a friend of ours, Joe, near his home south of Weatherford. A creek ran through his property and emptied into the Brazos. This time, my brother Eldon accompanied Dad and me; and the four of us were abreast, wading in the creek, looking for some deep holes where we might find some fish. Where we were walking was alternating from ankle deep to knee deep, and we were not seeing any fish at all. Now this creek bottom was hard rock and covered with moss, slippery as a raw oyster. Joe was wearing some rubber boots that reached to just below his knees.

As we were cautiously making our way on this treacherous footing, spread out in a line so we would not miss seeing any fish, Joe suddenly said, "Hey, guys, I think I've got a fish in my boot!" We (my father, brother, and I) turned to look down at his boot with him, but it wasn't a fish's tail we saw sticking up out of his right boot—it was a *snake's*! Joe jumped about six feet in the air and slung his right foot another three feet higher, thus shedding that boot in a hurry. He then commenced to running and leaping down that slippery creek at about 9.2 speed, yelling "Oh! Oh! Oh!" at every step until Eldon caught and tackled him. Meanwhile, Dad, Eldon, and I were cracking our ribs from laughing so hard. It turned out that the snake *did* bite Joe, but it was only a water moccasin, and his toe only swelled a little bit.

Now I'm sure Joe had a different view of this incident for he did not laugh at all. Evidently, like my neighbor Mose in a previous story, Joe did not like snakes. Period.

# CHAPTER 11

# THE MEANEST TEACHER

Throughout our school years, we have all experienced different types of teachers. We certainly remember the easy teachers we had and the easy grades we acquired from them. On the other hand, we also remember the hard teachers we took in school. For me, that would be my plane geometry teacher when I was a junior in high school. Seriously, that man ate nails and spat out tacks. Now math was not my strong suit anyway, but I strove mightily to master plane geometry. Our instructor used a teaching tool of writing a problem on the board and offering a brand-new penny to anyone who would come and solve it. I would always enthusiastically raise my hand and sprint to the board, eager to earn that penny. Any guesses as to how many pennies I earned in his class in that one year? Kudos to you if you guessed zero! I could have worked that very problem the night before in my geometry notebook, but at the chalkboard, my mind would go blank or numb.

I became the joke of the class. He would put a problem on the board, my hand would shoot up first, and he would reluctantly sigh, "Okay, Weldon, go ahead and try." Again, my attempt would end in failure. Now my older brother Eldon earned about two piggy banks' full. Yet would you believe I made an *A* in that math teacher's class? Also that my geometry notebook is on display in the museum on the first floor of the Guinn Justice Center right now? Miracles will never cease.

However, that high school math teacher was not the meanest teacher that I ever had; he was just the toughest and most demanding. About ten years after I had graduated, I returned for our homecoming game. We were sitting around at the country club that Friday night before the game the next day, and the subject of the meanest teacher came up. I said, "Shoot, that's no contest. My meanest teacher was my first-grade teacher at Santa Fe Elementary, Ms. Krouse." She kept a ruler and a paddle handy and utilized them both often. I sometimes thought that she spanked me every other day just to keep her arm in shape. Now naturally, my point of view could be slightly prejudiced and exaggerated, but I honestly don't remember her spanking anyone else but me that entire year! Plus one time, she spanked me when I was totally innocent.

Buffalo Creek meandered along just behind the school, and there was a large water or sewage pipe running across it. Sometimes at recess, we boys would attempt to walk across it and back just to show off in front of all the girls. Well, on this one occasion, I had successfully made it across; but on the way back, I lost my balance and began falling. Rather than just falling sideways into the water, I was able to twist and land feet first. Fortunately, the water depth only reached my thighs, but still there was a lot of laughter aimed at me by all my friends. Embarrassed, to say the least, I trudged my way to Ms. Krouse's classroom, who was waiting at the door to greet all of her kids.

When she saw my wet pants, she exclaimed, "Weldon Reed, you peed your pants!" After saying that, she grabbed me by the wrist, dragged me to her desk, and got out her large wooden paddle. Usually, Ms. Krouse, when a spanking was about to take place, would take the child back to the privacy of the cloakroom. However, this time, she commenced to whale the dickens out of me right there in front of the whole class, with me screaming bloody murder the whole time.

As I told this story to my friends sitting around our table at the country club that Friday night, one of them said, "Weldon, Ms. Krouse is in the hospital there on North Main."

"What? She's still alive?" I exclaimed. "Why, she was older than Methuselah when I had her!"

Well, Saturday morning, before the homecoming game that afternoon, I decided to go visit her, so I drove to the hospital and went inside. Asking for her room number, I went up to the second floor and stopped in front her room.

I timidly knocked on her door. (Would you believe I still had some trepidation regarding seeing her?)

Then I heard this quavering little voice say, "Come in."

I did so, and I still recognized this frail little form with gray hair, lying on the bed. I slowly approached her and took one of her little emaciated hands in mine, just about speechless.

Finally, I got up enough nerve to say, "Ms. Krouse, you probably won't remember me, but I had you for first grade about twenty years ago. I'm Weldon Reed."

"Oh, yes," she replied. "You're that sweet little Reed boy."

"Uh, no, ma'am," I responded. "I'm afraid you're confusing me with my older brother Eldon. He was in your class two years before me. I was the little freckled-faced one."

"Oh, I remember you now," she answered.

There was an awkward silence for some seconds there as I was desperately thinking of something to say, and as I was holding her hand, I blurted out, "You know, Ms. Krouse, I didn't remember you having hands when I was in your class."

She exclaimed, "Well, 'lands, child, whatever do you mean?"

I replied, "I just remember a ruler and a paddle!"

Fortunately, she had a good sense of humor for she just laughed and laughed. However, I then thanked her for each and every spanking for I richly deserved them (except for that one). At that age, I was just a little hellion, like a number of six-year-old males. That is why my heart goes out to all those poor first-grade teachers who have to educate and discipline today's male first graders without being able "to apply the *board* of education to the *seat* of learning." What a herculean (and mostly thankless) task!

# CHAPTER 12

# DELIGHTFUL DAYS ON A DAIRY

Ever had the privilege of working on a dairy? Hats off to those people—you talk about demanding! Between the ages of fourteen to sixteen, during the summers, I would spend ten days to two weeks on a dairy in Godly. My sister's husband had a younger brother named Kenneth who was my age, and Kenneth's mother and stepdad owned this dairy. The daily routine was pretty much you would work "from can to can't" ("from can see to can't see"). We would get up at about five-thirty in the morning and get dressed. As we walked through the kitchen, headed toward the back door, Kenneth's mom would hand us a slice of bread, rolled up with a slice of bologna in it, and we would munch on that on the walk down to the barn. There, we would wash that mini-breakfast down with a dipper full of the coldest milk ever from ten-gallon cans stored in ice-cold water vats. Then Kenneth and I would pull our pouches of Beechnut chewing tobacco out of our back pockets, put a big wad in one of our cheeks, and the workday would commence.

Kenneth's stepfather owned about sixty cows, mostly Holsteins and a few Jerseys. We would work them about thirty at a time. The milk barn had fifteen stalls on each side, with a long feeding trough running the length of each side, into which we had dumped about a half-gallon of feed in each stall. We would let the first thirty cows in, and to me, it was always remarkable that each cow knew which stall to stick her head in, and she would start munching away. Then one of us—Kenneth, his mother, his stepdad, and I—would step in beside the cows, slide this vertical board over that would hold the cows' heads in, and bolt them in. We would then place these round, enclosed milking buckets underneath the cows. Each bucket had four cylindrical suckers attached, and the buckets were held there by leather straps. We would then slip the four cylindrical suckers on each teat, letting the electrical power do the work. After the machine had done its work, most of the cows we would have to strip (finishing milking by hand into a pail).

A few of the cows had a tendency to kick, and we would put metal hobbles on their back legs as a prevention. I remember on one occasion Kenneth's mom was carrying a full pail to the back to empty and brushed the rear of this one cow that we did not have hobbled. It lashed out a hoof and hit the milk pail, flattening it and knocking her across the aisle into another cow, who promptly kicked her back the other way. Needless to say, Kenneth's mom became somewhat upset and commenced to whaling the dickens out of both cows with the flattened milk pail. Kenneth's stepdad had to calm her down.

After finishing those thirty cows, we ran them out and repeated the routine with the other thirty. After those thirty were milked came the fun part. Sixty cows left an immense amount of manure, which we had to push down to the open back end of the barn using these long-handled scrapers. Oh, what fun! Then we shoveled all of that into wheelbarrows and dumped it into the manure pile some distance from the barn. Then we hosed the floor down and sprinkled white lime all over it. That finished the milking for the morning until we had to repeat the same delightful routine that afternoon around four o'clock.

After the morning chore was finished, it was now around eight-thirty or nine, and we would head back to the house for a larger breakfast, usually consisting of fried eggs or scrambled, gravy, biscuits, and, believe it or not, fried bologna. Guess what we would have for lunch? Bologna sandwiches! It's a good thing I liked bologna, and still do. Now after breakfast, there ordinarily was more farm work, like mending fences, hauling hay, dehorning cows, plowing, etc.

If Kenneth and I had some free time (which actually did occur now and then), we had a number of options. We would go zipping around the pastures on his two-seater Cushman motor scooter, usually risking life and limb as we flew down gullies, and up and down small hills. We also would carry with us Kenneth's single-shot .22 and either try to shoot jackrabbits on the fly, by whoever was riding in the back seat, or stop and jump off and shoot them (usually missing). However, I remember on one occasion when I suggested something we could do that wound up getting us in trouble with his stepfather.

He had six or seven yearling calves in a pen adjacent to the barn. They were fair sized, weighing about three or four hundred pounds, perfect size, I thought, for riding them rodeo style. Naturally, they did not have saddles or bridles, or anything to hold on to; so once we finally cornered one and one of us got up on its back, we didn't stay up there long but went flying everywhere. It just so happened that I had acquired a pack of cigarettes (I'll never tell how), and we commenced to light up, just like real cowboys. After smoking a couple and relaxing, sitting on the top fence rail, around the corner of the barn walked his stepdad. To put it mildly, he was not happy that we were smoking that close to the barn and expressed his displeasure. I immediately confessed to him that it was my idea and my cigarettes, and that Kenneth just went along with me. Kenneth's stepdad slowly started removing his belt and said, "Weldon, I can't whip you for you're our guest, but I'm going to whip Kenneth. Plus, I'm then going to whip him a *second* time for you."

Ouch! You talk about a whipping hurting me and I didn't even receive it! But one thing I can say about Kenneth—he never whimpered or cried during either whipping and didn't hold it against me either. He was that good a friend and that tough a boy. "Those were the days, my friend."

# CHAPTER 13

# DADDY VERSUS ANIMALS

I bet my daddy did something that your daddy did not do nor would ever do. Surely most of us, at one time or another while driving a car, have swerved to miss a skunk on the road. However, I can honestly testify, having witnessed it myself when I was about ten or twelve, that Daddy did something quite unique, if not absolutely unheard of. He drove *off* the road and down into a shallow ditch to *hit* a skunk, not miss it. When we were traveling anywhere, Daddy simply looked at four-legged critters as moving targets. He would sometimes keep a running record of his score as we were driving along. Since we did not have air conditioning in our car then (it being about 1950 or so), Daddy had his window down and would just reach his hand out and mark the score on the dirty door—"1 rabbit, 2 squirrels, 1 skunk, 1 dillo" (short for armadillo), etc.

I really do not need to discuss the demises of various pets of ours who ran afoul of Daddy, but there were a couple that he did tolerate. One was Billy. One night, Mom and Daddy had been out that night with some friends of ours from across the street there on Sabine, Willard and Teeny ("Teeny" was short for "Tennessee"). I heard our car pull up in the driveway, and in they walked through the door. Daddy told me, "Weldon, go get that goat out of the back seat and tie him to the clothesline." (I prefer not to discuss why a goat was in the back seat of our car. I'll just leave that to your imagination.)

Anyway, when Daddy said jump, I would ask how high on the way up, meaning, I obeyed him instantly. I knew there was going to be a goat in the back seat, so I strolled out to the car and opened the back door. Sure enough, there stood a goat with a cotton rope around his neck, about a thousand black pellets all over the seat and floor, and a stench that watered your eyeballs. I pulled him out of the car and led him to the backyard to our clothesline. There, I tied him to one of the two wires stretching between the two poles and went back in the house. Now being the curious sort, I had to ask Daddy how he came by this goat, and Daddy said he had won him on a bet. Remember those red bottles of hot sauce you would find on café tables and other place's tables? Well, Daddy bet this man five dollars that he could drink the whole bottle and never bat an eyelash, and certainly wouldn't cry. The man replied that he didn't have five dollars, but he would bet this goat that he had in the back of his pickup. Naturally, Daddy took him up on it, and that was why he had a goat in his back seat.

The next morning early, I went to gather eggs, and Billy (that's what I named the goat) was gone—rope and all! He had apparently eaten through the rope (it being made of cotton) and took off. I immediately started running around the neighborhood looking for him and shortly found him less than a block away, calmly munching on a neighbor's roses (rather expensive roses too for he charged Daddy five dollars' worth of damages or he would keep the goat). I thought for sure that Daddy would just wash his hands of that goat, but unbelievably, he paid the money; and we took Billy home. Thereafter, we chained him up and dared him to eat that chain. One thing Daddy liked about that worthless goat was that it liked cigarettes. No, not to smoke but to eat. Daddy would feed him one of his Luckies and laugh every time Billy would gobble it down. If the cigarette were the last one in the pack, Daddy would then feed it the *pack* too, and Billy would eat that as well.

Something else that Daddy liked about that goat was the fighting that would go on between it and our dog Blackie, an old shepherd. Daddy tolerated having Blackie around because he was a good watchdog. Anyway, somewhere in Blackie's heritage, he had learned how to handle a goat. He would start chasing Billie, run up alongside of it, and grab the goat's chin whiskers in his teeth. Then he would abruptly sit down and turn that goat head over heels in the prettiest somersault you ever saw. Now Billy did not appreciate the trick, but Daddy and I would die laughing. Finally, Billy just became too much trouble to put up with. Plus, I guess he was costing Daddy too many cigarettes, so we gave him to some friends who lived out on the Covington road.

However, Daddy's favorite animal to tolerate, so to speak, was our cat, Mousey. We moved to Cleburne in 1945, when I was four years old, and that's when we got Mousey and had her for fourteen years. She was grey like a mouse, hence her name. Daddy liked her because she lived up to her name—she was a mouser and a half. In addition, which really tickled Daddy, she was an absolute terror to most dogs. She would put them on the run and chase them down the street.

One time in particular, Mousey had a litter of kittens (I believe she cat-populated most of northeast Cleburne for she would have two or three litters a year). Anyway, Mother had set the apple crate containing Mousey and her kittens on the front porch to air for a while. Daddy and I were sitting on the steps while he was working on a carburetor, and we noticed a neighborhood dog, just an old brown mutt, trotting along on the other side of the street. Now he had no more idea than the man in the moon that Mousey was around, and he certainly did not know that she was also guarding her kittens on the front porch. Suddenly, this gray streak of lightning shot off the porch and pounced on the back of that dog with claws just a ripping away. Off he dashed, with tufts of brown hair flying everywhere, and him yelping his head off like the devil himself were after him (which was probably true—a feline version anyway). Again, Daddy and I died laughing.

Yes, indeed, Billy the goat and Mousey the cat were special and privileged in that they both earned Daddy's admiration and avoided arousing his wrath.

# CHAPTER 14

## MY PLAYGROUND—
## THE SANTA FE SHOPS

I suppose most kids in the '40s and '50s had a playground of some sort handy. I dare say the country club bunch even had one in their own backyard. Others probably lived close enough to an elementary school or the city park and could walk there. However, in my neighborhood, we were literally "the poor kids across the tracks."

The Santa Fe railroad tracks separated us from the rest of the town, so some of us ten or eleven-year-old kids made do with what was available to us—the Santa Fe shops.

Now the actual shops themselves (the machine shops, where the locomotives were constructed or rebuilt, or repaired) were not really close to my house on north Sabine Street. Those shops were down near the East Gate. That's where Mom and I would go to pick up Daddy when he got off work at six o'clock or later, if he worked a little overtime. They had a little waiting room of sorts right there at the gate where we would sit and wait. I could look out the window when we were driving up and see that 230-foot smokestack that Daddy once climbed to win a five-dollar bet. I wouldn't climb that thing for fifty thousand dollars. I have acrophobia, and that fear has struck me on various occasions (but that's another story for another time).

So what I broadly referred to as the shops was simply the area of the Santa Fe property directly behind my house, which was really primarily a storage area for stacks of railroad ties and a graveyard of old boxcars and flatcars in various stages of decay. These were wonderful places to search for anything to play with, or to play cowboys and Indians or cops and robbers. It was all up to our imagination. Ronnie, Caroll, and I would spend hours climbing in and out of those empty boxcars. Sometimes, we would find some metal junk, like railroad spikes or broken steering wheels that controlled the brakes for each boxcar, and those items we could sell to my Uncle O. B., the one who owned the junkyard at the corner of Sabine and Boone Streets. From time to time, we would find some sulfur rocks, which, when we set them in a fire, would burn with this weird yellowish-green blaze. I found out later (much later) that that could have killed us because the first time we burned some, we did so in our cave that we had dug underground in an empty lot. The cave had a canvas flap on one end of the ceiling, which served as our doorway, offering poor ventilation, and the sulfur dioxide gas could have suffocated us. Oh, well, that was just par for the course for some of us. It's a wonder we survived those years.

However, we still had more things we could do in our playground. For example, we would stand on top of the overpass on Boone

Street and try to drop rocks down the smokestacks of the locomotives as they passed underneath, or even more exciting, climb down beside the tracks under the overpass and throw rocks at the engineers or conductors as the trains passed. We did hear a bit of cussing from time to time, but what can I say? I guess we were Cleburne's version of the Little Rascals or the Bowery Boys, whom we saw in the movies.

Some more entertainment involved the holding pens that the Santa Fe had about a half a mile or so north of the Boone overpass. Occasionally, the trains would drop off or pick up various groups of livestock held there in those pens; but before the cows, calves, or goats were picked up, we had the opportunity to play with them. (For some reason, I do not remember the Santa Fe keeping any horses there. Of course, that could also be my memory failing me, as it sometimes does. However, when that occurs, I usually just make things up.) Anyway, these available animals provided us with our very own rodeo—and free to boot! How many well-to-do kids could say that? I remember on one occasion that a bunch of goats were awaiting our pleasure. (Nowadays, young kids at the rodeos participate in "mutton bustin'." What in the heck can I call goat riding? Cabrito conquering? Goat vanquishing? Cabrito clobbering? Goat quelling? It does seem to lose something there in the translation, doesn't it? You know, this writing gig can be a bit of a chore.) Oh, well, back to the story.

Ronnie, Caroll, and I would hem a goat up in a corner, and then one of us would hop on and feebly attempt to ride 'em for those eight seconds. It was about like trying to stay on a greased pig because we would slide off after two seconds and go rolling like a tumbleweed. I was just standing there, watching Caroll try to hang to one nanny goat, when Ronnie suddenly yelled, "Look out, Weldon!" I jerked around to see what was going on when I got a brief glimpse of this brown blur barreling right at me. A big old ram slammed into my stomach, knocking me about three feet backward and into the wooden fencing that comprised the pen. Luckily for me, Ronnie had come running up and got between me and the ram, or it might have continued to butt me senseless. (I know what you're thinking—I didn't have any sense!)

A last dangerous game we would play on our playground was hoboing, "riding the rails." Once the train had dropped off some live-stock or picked some up, if it were headed north, toward Joshua, we would sometimes climb up in an open boxcar and ride it to that next little town about ten miles up. There, the train would slow down to pass through the western edge of town, and we would jump off and start walking back to Cleburne. We never chose to wait for a southbound train; that could have been hours later. We preferred to just stroll back to Cleburne, searching the ground on both sides of the tracks to see if we could find something interesting, like a half-smoked cigar or old whiskey bottle with some amber liquid still in it that we would finish off.

Hey, didn't most kids do fun stuff like that?

# CHAPTER 15

# THE PUNY PUGILIST

When I graduated from sixth grade at Irving Elementary School, I entered seventh grade at dear old Fulton Junior High. There, I made many new friends and some who became very dear to me. Two of them were Rex and Bobby. Rex was in my homeroom at Fulton, and we hit it off instantly. We were both just good old country boys, easy to get along with, but there were five other boys in our homeroom that Rex and I did not quite cotton to. They were a little on the uppity side, probably lived on the west and south side of town, where the more well to do dwelled. As I have indicated before, I literally lived "across the tracks," so these snooty guys didn't appeal to me and Rex at all.

One day at recess, Rex and I had a run-in with this bunch. He and I were leaning up against the wire screen behind home plate on the baseball field when these five boys came strolling by. I really do not remember who said what to whom, but Rex definitely got ticked off about something and yelled at them, "Weldon and I will take on all five of you at the same time. Come on at us and take your licking!" Please notice that Rex had not asked me if I would be willing to side with him; he just volunteered me. Naturally, I couldn't back down, so here they came. Now these other five boys and I were about the same size. Rex, however, was a couple of inches taller and about ten pounds heavier. You tell me—would you want to trade punches with Rex or with me if you were one of those five? One or two would dart in at Rex, throw a quick punch, and then jump back out. Meanwhile, the other three were standing in front of me, whaling away. In about a minute flat, my nose was bleeding, and my lips were swelling up. Thank the Good Lord Rex saw my predicament, slid over in front of me, and commenced to pound the dickens out of those that stayed within punching range, thus saving what was left of my handsome face. There was another significant time that Rex aided me, but I will save that for a later date since it occurred when we were juniors in high school.

My other best friend, Bobby, and I were two lucky boys. We met in eighth grade, and we both landed the cushiest summer job two kids could ever have. We were hired as buckle boys at the public skating rink down at the city park. The job itself was easy enough. There were two skating sessions on Friday and Saturday nights during the summer, and all we had to do was to buckle the leather straps around the ankles and across the top of the toes of whoever needed our help. Usually, it was primarily girls we helped, which was really a sacrifice on mine and Bobby's part, getting to flirt with each and every one. The buckling task would only take about five or six minutes of each session, and then we were free to skate the rest of the time on our own. In addition, the job also came with a free summer pass to the swimming pool. Bobby and I were the envy of a bunch of guys in junior high.

However, one night, some trouble occurred. There was another eighth grader skating, named Bruton, who was bullying anyone smaller than him and trying to start a fight. Now this would have been about 1955. Back then, if you failed a grade, you actually had to stay in that grade until you passed it (Oh, the horror!) or quit school totally. I know Bruton had failed at least two grades and possibly even three, so he was eight to ten inches taller than any of us other eighth graders and probably outweighed us fifteen to twenty pounds. Thus as my luck would have it, here he skates up to me and says, "Come on, Reed. Step outside the rink and I'll pound you to a pulp."

I just replied, "Bruton, go pick on someone your own size," and skated away. He then challenged Bobby too, and Bobby just ignored him and skated over to where I was standing by the fence. We then watched Bruton sort of circle the rink, jawing at every little guy there. I was getting madder by the minute and finally had had enough. I told Bobby, "Why don't you and I challenge him, see if he's brave enough to take us both on at the same time?"

Now I will admit Bobby was a little hesitant there (he had better sense than I did), but he said, "Let's go." We skated over to Bruton and challenged him, saying we both would fight him if he had the guts to step outside. He just laughed and began taking off his skates. We followed suit, along with a number of other guys who wanted to watch the fight (which shouldn't last long, as I kept noticing that Bruton's arms were about a foot longer that mine or Bobby's. Oh, well, as long as I could land a punch or two.) The lighting outside the rink was a little on the dim side, but we three squared off, and the punches started flying. Unfortunately for me and Bobby, they were just about all being landed by Bruton. In no time flat, my nose was bleeding, my lips were puffy, and my ears were ringing. (Does this sound familiar? Yep, just like the fight standing beside Rex!).

I didn't like the way this was going at all, so I called, "Time out," and Bobby and I huddled up. I said, "Listen, this long-distance punching is not working at all. Let's both charge him and try to get him down on the ground. I haven't even landed one punch."

Bobby said, "Well, I haven't either, so let's do it."

I yelled to Bruton, "Time in," and Bobby and I charged him. As we barreled into Bruton, down we, all three, went, rolling about on the ground. When the dust settled, my friend Bobby wound up on the bottom, facing upward; Bruton was in the middle, facing upward; and I was on top, facing downward. Boy, now was my chance! I was going to land at least one big blow on him, so I drew back my right fist and plunged it downward with all my strength. Just as it was about to land on Bruton's nose, hopefully knocking it clean off, he jerked his head aside, and my fist busted Bobby right in the eye! Oh, no!

Naturally, Bobby yelled out, and then suddenly, somebody grabbed me by the shoulders and jerked me to my feet. It was the skating rink manager, who then yanked Bruton to his feet and told him to leave the premises immediately, for the manager knew he was always the troublemaker. Meanwhile, Bobby slowly climbed to his feet, holding his hand over his eye and groaning. He said to me, "Boy, Weldon, Bruton really popped me one there at the end."

Do you think I was going to be crazy enough to confess to Bobby that I did it? In that dim light, if he thought Bruton had hit him, I wasn't going to tell him otherwise for that could have ended a friendship, if not my life! However, I did gain the courage to tell Bobby the truth—some fourteen years later when we were both married and had children!

# CHAPTER 16

# DADDY AND DISCIPLINE

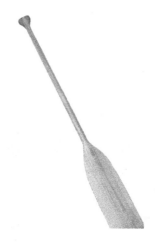

Beyond question, the Child Protective Services would have arrested Daddy if that organization had been in existence back then. Daddy was definitely "old school" as was just about every father that I knew of back in the '40s and '50s. Looking back, I would not in any way question Daddy's right to do so, nor would I question the reality that I deserved every "whupping" (Daddy did not spank or switch) that he administered.

Now there was *one* occasion when Daddy whipped me, and I really did not deserve it. It was on my birthday when I had just turned seven. We had friends and relatives over for the party. The adults were in the living room visiting, and we kids were outside in the front yard playing a rather innocent game that we boys liked to play. It involved our standing in a circle, and one of us attempting to throw a butter knife so that it stuck in the ground as close to someone's foot as possible. (I know, I know, it sounds like a silly game, but hey, it was entertaining to us!) Now my friend Ronnie had thrown the butter knife at my foot, so now it was my turn to throw. Unfortunately for me, I was facing our living room window, and just as I brought my arm forward, the butter knife slipped out of my hand and crashed through our living room window, where all of the adults were seated. Now you tell me—would I have done that *on purpose* with Daddy in that living room?

Knowing my dad as I do, I immediately ran around the side of the house where there was an opening in the foundation siding. I dropped down and crawled under the house as far back as I could go, right amongst the spider webs. I was hoping that Daddy, as mad as he was going to be, would not want to crawl back there. I lay there, trembling, fearing for my very life, when I saw Daddy's head poke into the hole. "Weldon Thomas, come out of there," he yelled.

"No, Daddy; you'll whip me, and it was an accident."

"No, I won't," he replied. "Now come on out of there before I really get mad."

Since I certainly did not want to see him "really mad," I crawled out, protesting my innocence every foot of the way to no avail. Would you believe he whipped me right in front of my cousins and friends, and it was certainly more than seven and one to grow on?

On another occasion, Daddy applied another form of discipline simply because I was not paying sufficient attention to his voice. When I was about ten, we were having a Reed reunion down at the city park. About ten or so cousins and I were running around like chickens with our heads cut off, chasing one another and yelling, having the time of our life. I do remember hearing an adult voice yelling something somewhere, but it could not possibly be anyone calling me, so I ignored it. I continued running around when suddenly, *bam*! Something hit me on the back of the head, knocking me flat on my face in the dirt. I groggily got to my hands and knees, and there on the ground was the object that had struck me. My dad had brained me with a horse apple from about forty yards away! Drat him. It was just my bad luck that Daddy had pitched some semipro ball in Oklahoma and Texas when he was rough necking.

One last memorable disciplinary act of my dad's I richly deserved. Can I help it if I failed to master my "impulse of the moment" occurrence? As I walked around the corner of the house (again about the age of ten), I saw Daddy working on his '50 Chevy. With the hood up, he was bent over, fiddling with something. All I could think of was "what a target" his derriere made for my slingshot, which I just so happened to have in my hand, already loaded with a marble-sized rock. Naturally, I fired away, drilling him dead center. The impact caused him to jump straight up, knocking the hood off its support rod, and the hood hit him a second time on the way down. He slowly turned around; flames were shooting from his eyes and smoke from his ears. I knew my time had come, so I just threw myself down, groveling at his feet, begging him not to kill me. Well, he did kill me—this is my ghost writing this.

# CHAPTER 17

## A SMORGASBORD OF INHERENT IGNORANCE

I don't know what the connection was, but for some reason, a good percentage of my demonstrations of innate stupidity involved animals or my Uncle O. B., or both. For example, late one evening, when I was about eight, Uncle O. B. stopped by our house right after Daddy got in from work; and he was visiting with us in our living room. I did not notice that one of his hands was closed until he called me over and said, "Bullfrog, here is a gift for you. Hold out your hand." I did so, and he opened up his hand and rolled into mine four of the tiniest eggs I had ever seen, about the size of an average round jellybean. He told me they were banty eggs, and if I were to set them, they would hatch for they were fertilized. Now remember that I was only eight—how was I to know the difference between "set" and "sat"? So before Mom or Dad could say or do anything, I promptly placed them on the footstool in front of Mom's chair and "sat" on them. Yes, the customary result occurred—Daddy whipped me for being so dimwitted. Also, of course, I had to scrub the mess off Mom's footstool.

On another occasion, at about the same age, I was visiting at Uncle O. B.'s house, watching him cut a fender off one of his junk cars that he had just hauled in from somewhere. Using his acetylene cutting torch, he had sparks flying everywhere, which always fascinated me. It was summer time and hot, so Uncle O. B. suggested we take a break and go into his house for some ice water. That sounded good to me, so we traipsed into the house, and he poured us both a glass from his water pitcher in his icebox (a *real* icebox, the type where you put a block of ice in the top of it. Some of y'all remember). Then we sat down on the back porch steps to drink them before he went back to work. After a while, he asked me something, "Bullfrog, have you ever drunk any goat's milk?"

I answered, "No, I'm pretty sure Mom has never bought us any. Why?"

"Well," he replied, "if you drink goat's milk, your head gets hard like a goat's, and you could butt a door down or knock over a small tree."

"Really?" I asked. "Darn, I sure wish Mom would buy some sometime. I'd like to try that."

Uncle O. B. smiled real big and said, "Son, you are in luck. I happen to have some in the icebox. Wait here and I'll bring you a glass."

Boy, I was thinking, "What a great uncle I have to keep neat stuff around like wonderful goat's milk."

Then Uncle O. B. stepped out the back door with a glass of milk in his hand and said, "Here it is. Drink 'er down." Immediately, I grabbed the glass and drained it; although to me, it didn't taste any different from cow's milk. However, Uncle O. B. said, "Now feel the top of your head. Isn't it getting a little harder already?"

I put my right hand up there and rubbed it around, and sure enough, it did seem to be harder than before. "Yes, Unc, I think your right," I excitedly responded.

"All right," he stated, "let's give it a try. Draw a bead on my back door there and ram it." The door was about six feet from where I was sitting, so I got to my feet and charged. *Bam!* Naturally, the impact knocked me backward onto my rear; and as I groggily got to my feet, I told my uncle that I didn't think the goat's milk worked because my head was ringing, and I was seeing stars. Of course, the experiment was semi-successful for I did feel a small knob on my head. Was that the beginning of a small goat horn?

Another animal episode I could actually blame on going to the movies. I was about twelve, and on a Saturday morning, I walked downtown to see a show with a couple of friends. I don't remember if we went to the Texas Theater or the Yale, but we always liked to see the "B" westerns. Bob Steele, Lash LaRue, Whip Wilson, the Durango Kid, Tim Holt and his sidekick Chito (you remember him, with the three middle names and a last name of Rafferty), the Cisco Kid and Pancho (remember their horses' names?)—you name 'em; I loved them all, especially Bob Steele, who could fight four or five guys at the same time, whip them all, and never get his hat knocked off. It was amazing! Anyway, this particular movie was preceded with a ten-minute special about a different type of cowboys—the South American gauchos from Argentina and Brazil. These guys would rope cows with something called a bola. It consisted of three three-foot strips of leather with a round, leather-covered ball filled with rocks on the end of each strip. The strips were tied together at one end, with the round rocks hanging at the other end. The gaucho would chase after a cow on horseback, and when he got close enough, he would whirl that bola in a circle over his hand, usually just one rotation, and then release it right at the cow's legs. The round balls would wrap themselves around that cow's legs, and it would tumble.

That particular stunt really captured my imagination, and when I got home, my vivid (and sometimes demented) imagination started firing on all cylinders (okay, maybe on just one cylinder). How could I duplicate the feat of those gauchos? We didn't have any cows nor a horse either, so there went that idea. Aha! Inspiration struck! We did have chickens! All right, my next challenge was to manufacture some sort of bola. Trying to make a round bola out of leather-bound rocks seemed like too much trouble. There had to be a simpler way. Then an idea occurred to me—Daddy had a bunch of odds and ends stuff in the storage shed that I could tie together. So I ambled out to the shed and began looking around. Sure enough, I found some large bolts with big nuts on the end; each nut was about one inch in diameter. Three of those tied together with cord should do the trick on chicken legs, as thin as those legs were.

In about ten minutes, my homemade bola was ready, and out to the chicken pen I went. I immediately started chasing one Rhode Island Red hen, whirled the bola over my head, and tossed it right at her legs. Eureka! I was successful! Down the hen went in a heap, but when I reached her and unwound the bola, I noticed a slight problem (well, actually, a major problem—one of her legs was dangling off to the side, broken). Oops! Hey, not even Thomas Edison was successful the first time, so I confidently tried a second time with another hen. Darn! Same result! Now my enthusiasm was really waning, and a larger problem loomed before me. How was I going to explain to Daddy about how those two hens wound up with broken legs? Of course, he was going to question me first; and if he did not buy my story (which he rarely did—Daddy was hard to fool), the black belt would come out of Daddy's closet. Did I mention that this belt was not one you would purchase at J. C. Penney's but was one that the barbers used to whet their straight razors? That fate awaited me if I did not come up with the story of a lifetime.

Well, believe it or not, I did come up with the story of a lifetime. When Daddy pulled into the driveway, coming from work, I ran out the door to meet him and tell him the news. "Daddy! Daddy! I heard the chickens squawking a while ago and ran out to the chicken pen. There was a big, black dog in there chasing them around and jumped on a couple of them. I grabbed a stick there lying beside the storage shed and ran into the chicken pen, swinging away at that dog. He flew toward the other end of the pen and climbed over the fence quicker than you could blink! Luckily, he hadn't had time enough to kill any or eat them, although there are a couple of hens he seemed to have crippled."

Daddy started walking over to the pen, and I followed him. He could see the hens hobbling around. Meanwhile, my heart was pounding out of my chest; my very life hung in the balance. Daddy just turned to me and said, "Good job, son. Next time, grab the .22 out of the closet if you have time and shoot the blamed thing. Now we'll just have to eat those hens sooner than I had planned on."

If you can't be good, be lucky—or slick.

# CHAPTER 18

# MY GRANPA REED

When I was ten or so, in the early 1950s, Granpa Reed lived in Rio Vista (pronounced "Ri Visty") with his two spinster sisters, Aunt Betty and Aunt Bessie. Aunt Betty was a rather thin, quiet lady, and Aunt Bessie was rather hefty and dipped snuff. I thought that was rather unsightly for a woman especially when seeing the thin trickle of brown dripping down each side of her mouth. Now Granpa dipped too, but that was okay for he was a man. However, the way he put the snuff behind his lip was unique, I thought. Most men take a pinch between their thumb and forefinger, pull out their lower lip with the other hand, and place the snuff there. Granpa did it differently. He had an Old Timer's knife, one with two blades (large and small). He would open his can of Garrett's snuff and then open his knife and insert the small blade. Then he would carefully remove the knife from the can, with the blade now having a thin strip of snuff on it. Let me point out that that blade was sharp enough to shave steel. Thus, I always watched Granpa with anticipation, anxiously looking for him to sever his lower lip and watching it fall to the floor or ground—never happened. It was a wonder.

Granpa's house was a little different too. He had a one-holer outdoor john (which was okay for we had one too at our house on Sabine Street); however, ours was a two holer, one small and one large. He had a wood-burning stove, and he and my aunts had no indoor water; they would carry water in from the well outside. They kept their drinking water in a bucket on the screened-in back porch with a dipper in it. In addition, walking to the well or to the out-house proved adventurous for Granpa had the meanest game rooster in the world, and he would attack anything that entered his territory. Now we youngsters could outrun it or kick it like a football, but Granpa, being in his upper sixties, was already having to use a cane to walk. However, he would use the cane as a weapon against the rooster. Actually, he had already cracked the cane once, whacking the fowl on the head, but he had wrapped bailing wire around it at the weak area (bailing wire was the duct tape of its era).

One of Granpa's favorite hobbies at the time was playing dominoes in downtown Rio Vista. There was a pavilion there in the center of the square (and it is still there). Several of Granpa's old cronies would meet him there where they would gather around this table to play some serious dominoes—and I do mean serious. The only talking or noise making permitted was done by the four men seated at the table. If there were any kids present (like me), we were to be seen and not heard. We could not run around like chickens with their heads cut off, screaming and laughing. Each of these four gentlemen carried canes, and none of them hesitated to bop an offensive child in the head. Another serious element in dominoes, at least to Granpa, was the fact that he grew his fingernail on his right index finger to a full one inch in length just to make it easier to rake in the dominoes.

Something else that Granpa took seriously was baseball, as did my dad. Both were pitchers in their younger days. The story goes that Granpa was even offered a semi-pro contract at one time, but Grandma Reed would not let him sign it but instead told him he had to continue working in the oil fields and help raise the two kids they already had (with eight more to follow). Daddy also was a pretty good pitcher, left handed, and he had done some pitching in the Army. Remember those booths at the carnivals where you knocked dolls off the shelves or knocked down milk bottles? After Daddy had won three or four of their largest stuffed dolls, the men running the booths would not let him pitch anymore. I saw that happen at the Alvarado Reunion several times. During this same time period, Daddy would pitch occasionally with this amateur team in the area.

One particular game took place at a field in Rio Vista. When the opposing team arrived, there was a slight problem—the umpire had not showed up yet. The teams only used one, behind home plate to call balls and strikes, and make any other call from there if he could (like somebody stealing second). One of the other team's players saw my grandfather sitting in the stands and suggested using him, even though my daddy was pitching for the home team. Granpa was evidently noted for his honesty, and they trusted him to call an objective game. So Granpa borrowed a spare catcher's mask, squatted behind the play, and yelled, "Play ball!" After several innings had passed, some trouble began brewing. Daddy thought Granpa was calling too objective of a game. He decided that Granpa was "squeezing" him (a baseball term, meaning the umpire's strike zone was rather small). Therefore, Daddy began barking some unkind comments in Granpa's direction, and Granpa barked right back. Now I was sitting in the stands with my mom, and I could not quite hear the exact comments flowing back and forth between the two, but Granpa had evidently reached his boiling point. He jumped up, jerked off his mask, and charged the mound. Please remember that Granpa was in his upper sixties, Daddy in his lower forties. Good grief! I was about to witness a fistfight between my dad and my grandfather! (Short tempers sort of ran in the Reed family). Fortunately, players from both sides were able to grab the two before blows were exchanged.

Another singular memory I have of Granpa occurred when he was in his mid-seventies; I was about sixteen. He was staying in one of those small hotels in Glen Rose that administered mineral baths. Granpa's arthritis had really been giving him fits, so he was staying there for a while. Every couple of weeks, Daddy and I would go over to visit him, making one stop on the way. Daddy knew of this bootlegger in Glen Rose who probably had the first drive-through liquor store. Daddy would pull up to this man's kitchen window, honk once, and the man would come to it and hand him a pint of whiskey in exchange for two dollars. We would then go pick up Granpa and take him to the pool hall in the middle of town, where he and Daddy would play some games while taking hits off the pint of whiskey. Those were some good memories.

# CHAPTER 19

# MY YEARS AS A PYROMANIAC

For some unexplainable reason during my years of being eight through twelve, I really experienced some serious cases of the dumbs, if you will. Nor was my Uncle O. B. involved either. I really did not need his help in demonstrating my innate idiocy from time to time. An impulse would strike, and off I would go, really not considering the consequences or possible disastrous outcomes especially when it came to matches or fire.

For example, when I was about eight, in third grade, I was walking home from Santa Fe Elementary shortly after New Year's. I was traipsing down Brazos Street at the time when I spotted a huge Roman candle lying in the gutter. It was about a foot-and-a-half long and as big around as the barrel of a baseball bat. Plus as an added attraction, it was open on one end, with powder spilling out. A sensational idea popped into my demented brain. "If I were to borrow a match from this man approaching, strike it and touch it to this powder, I bet it would blow up!" So lucky me, the man was a smoker and did have a match, which he handed to me. When I struck it and touched the powder with it, I discovered that I was absolutely correct—the Roman candle did explode. I saw a tremendous flash of light and then felt the most intense fiery pain in my right hand and face. I immediately began screaming, which attracted a lot of attention.

At that time in the '40s, there was a little café on Brazos at that location; and the owner, having seen what occurred, came running out with a stick of butter, which he generously applied to my face and hand. Luckily, all of my fingers were still attached (unlike that New York Giant football player recently), and of course, my face was badly burned. (Darn! There went my Hollywood-handsome good looks!) Several adults offered to drive me home, and I accepted a lift from the wife of the man who owned the café. When she dropped me off, she explained what had happened to Mother, and away to Dr. Little's we went (our family physician). He wiped off the butter and put a different ointment on me; he also suggested that I stay inside for a week or two, out of any sunlight and no playing outside. Well, my Grandma Bailey was a Licensed Vocational Nurse (LVN) and she lived in Denison, near the Oklahoma border. So off I went to her house for her to nurse me and—yippee! No school for a week or so!

Now you would have thought that I had learned my lesson about playing with matches from the Roman candle stunt, but no. Even at Grandma's house, temptation struck. She burned her trash in a fifty-five-gallon barrel sitting out by the alley in her backyard. Nearby, about six to eight feet away, was a telephone pole. A deranged thought struck me. What if I were to wrestle that barrel over to the telephone pole, pushing it right up against it, and light the trash inside it? Would the barrel get hot enough to burn or brand a mark on the pole? (I know what you're thinking. Surely, he would not be stupid enough to do that!) Okay, what does an eight-year-old know about creosote on telephone poles and its inflammatory nature? The barrel was only half-full of burnable trash, so I added some of Mr. Bailey's newspapers that nearly filled it up. (Mr. Bailey was Grandma's second husband, and for some reason, we never called him Grandpa, just Mr. Bailey.) Then I slipped into the kitchen where Grandma kept her matches in a metal container on the wall and snitched a couple.

Back at the barrel, I lit the trash and waited for the barrel to get hot. Boy, it got hot, all right—too hot! Suddenly, with a *swoosh*, the area of the pole against the barrel burst into flames instead of just leaving a burned mark! Uh-oh! This stunt is not going well. I ran into the house, yelling for Grandma and screaming that the telephone pole was on fire. By now, the flames were halfway up the pole, accompanied by plenty of smoke. Mr. Bailey ran back inside and called the fire department. Within minutes, they pulled up in the alley behind Grandma's house, dragged the fire hose into the backyard, and opened it up, extinguishing the flames rather quickly. Grandma then thanked the firemen, explaining to them that her grandson had burned the trash and "accidentally" set the pole on fire. After they left, while we were still in the backyard, the inquisition commenced. Who moved the barrel over up against the pole? Who then set the trash on fire? I was straining my brain, trying to come up with a believable lie (which I had been able to do so many times in the past), but I was stumped. My usual canny brain had let me down, and Grandma broke an appropriate switch from one of her trees in the backyard. Now her switchings never did compare to Daddy's whippings, but they were nothing to sneeze at. However, I did survive.

A couple of years later, catastrophe struck again. Grandma had given me a book of stories about young people getting into various kinds of trouble. One was about a girl who had told a teacher a lie; her mother found out about it and made the daughter eat a large, hot onion in front of her entire class with tears streaming down her face, both from the effects of the onion and her shame. Another story, though, really caught my attention for it dealt with a boy playing with matches. All right! A kindred spirit! This boy lived up north somewhere, and his family had a small, short storage shed in back that had a thatched roof, the kind made out of straw. He had the wonderful idea of selecting one of the pieces of straw that protruded the farthest, lighting it with a match, and then snatching the straw out and throwing it on the ground before it caught the others on fire. Isn't that sensational?

Now I had a problem—we had no thatched roof. However, there was an empty lot next to us, overgrown with weeds. I decided I could do something similar. I could light some of the grass on fire and see if I could stomp out the small fire before it got too big. The first two or three times I tried, I was successful in putting out the fire, but I got too daring on my fourth attempt and lost control of the blaze. So more yelling and screaming ensued as I ran into the house to tell Mom. She glanced out the window and called the fire department. Again, they arrived pretty quickly and drowned the fire; plus one of them lectured me rather sternly about playing with matches. Mother then marched me into the house and demonstrated another use for her hairbrush. Plus, I don't even need to mention what happened to me when Daddy got home from work. It wasn't pleasant.

Would you believe that last pyro episode still did not cure me from playing with fire? About a year later, I decided I would try the thatched roof gimmick again but this time on the wooden floor of our back porch. Instead of using straws or grass, I thought of inserting strips of paper torn from my Big Chief writing tablet into cracks in the porch floor, light them, and then pull them out and throw them on the ground when they got close to the boards. This, like the burning grass, worked fine the first couple of times I tried it, but the boards were very old and quite dry. Suddenly, the board itself caught on fire, and all my stomping could not put it out. Now both of the adjacent boards were burning fast, and I quickly ran yelling for Mom in the house. Another call to the fire department followed, with another lecture from a fireman, another spanking with the hairbrush from Mom, and later that evening, doomsday occurred when Daddy got home from work. However, there was a serendipity to this fiasco. Daddy not only built a new porch but also, he built Mom a new bedroom first and then added on the porch. Boy, what a lucky woman she was, right?

# CHAPTER 20

# HALLOWEEN HIJINKS

Trouble seemed to follow me even as I grew into my high school years, and I did not have to look for it. Consider, for example, Halloween night when I was a sophomore at Cleburne High and my older brother Eldon was a senior. He and I went out that night with some friends: Truitt Ownby, Ronnie Williams, and Jerry Walling (no, not the Jerry Walling that we all grew up with. This Jerry Walling was a friend of my brother's from Dallas who only attended Cleburne High his junior and senior year). We were in Truitt's parents' car, a grey 1956 Plymouth station wagon. Now this Plymouth was a V-8, and, brother, that thing could run. It sure proved it that night when we really needed it to.

We had some empty cardboard boxes sitting in the storage area behind the back seat where Eldon, Jerry, and I were sitting. We happened to know where the closest watermelon patch was, so we cruised out there south of town and helped ourselves to six or eight of them. (As Huck Finn said, we were only "borrowing" them.) Then we drove to the city park and commenced to break up the watermelons into chunks just right for throwing. After filling up the cardboard boxes, we drove up South Main to the courthouse and began circling it, occasionally leaning out the windows and chunking a few pieces at other teenagers that we knew who were walking by or driving by. As we were on the west side of the courthouse on Main Street, we happened to see a pickup full of guys about three blocks south who were slowly turning left, heading east on Harrel Street. Truitt quickly turned left at the alley one block south of the courthouse and sped to the corner of Caddo and parked. We were gambling that the pickup would turn north on Caddo and head back to circle the courthouse.

Sure enough, here they came. We had already piled out of Truitt's car and filled our hands with watermelon chunks, ready for our unsuspecting victims. We had not recognized the pickup or its occupants but believed they were some other guys from Cleburne. As they drew abreast of us, we five filled the air with watermelon missiles! Oops! Big mistake! It was a pickup load of fellas from Goatneck! Now those guys were rougher than a cob, and you did not want to mess with them. We dashed back to Truitt's car as the Goatneck boys jumped off their pickup and ran toward us. Truitt floorboarded the Plymouth. As he did so, one of the guys had reached the side of the car and thrust his hand through the back window, grabbing at whoever was sitting there, which happened to be my brother Eldon. He promptly punched the guy in the face, dropping him to the pavement. Truitt meanwhile sped past the pickup, heading north on Caddo and then turned west at the courthouse on Henderson. Here came the pickup, hot on our tail. Truitt figured we could easily out-run the pickup, so he slowed down some just to play with them.

When we reached Nolan River Road, Truitt turned south on it for a specific reason. It was still graveled back then (and was a popular parking spot to take your girl, by the way), so Truitt would let the pickup get right on his bumper and then speed up, showering it with gravel and especially the guys filling up the back of it. When we hit Country Club Road, Truitt was tired of toying with them, so we turned east on Country Club until we came to South Prairie. He then turned north on it until we reached West Henderson again, where we turned west, heading out of town on Highway 67. This time, Truitt put the pedal to the metal and flew down the highway with his speedometer bouncing off the 100 mph indicator. We quickly lost the pickup, and when we dropped down a hill, Truitt saw a side road angling off to the left, so he turned down it, doused the lights, and drifted to a stop. A minute passed, and then the pickup zoomed by, never seeing us.

We sat there for about an hour, and then figuring it was safe, Truitt started back up, and we drove back into town and began circling the courthouse once more. On the corner of Henderson and North Main, four or five girls started yelling and waving at us; so naturally, being typical boys, we pulled over and stopped to talk to them. Bad call! It was a trap! Up behind us sped a blue '56 Ford V-8 filled with Goatneck guys, and the race was on again; but this time, they had a fast car too. Truitt floorboarded the Plymouth again, heading west on Henderson and out on Highway 67 toward Glen Rose. However, we were not leaving our pursuers in the dust. They were sticking pretty close to us, but we gradually began pulling away until we had about a quarter-mile lead on them. Again, we dropped over this hill, and there again was the little gravel road angling off to the late. Once more, Truitt turned it down, cut off the lights, and drifted to a stop. Seconds later, the Ford flashed by, and our trick had worked again.

This time, we waited about an hour and a half before Truitt started back up, and we headed back to Cleburne. We had gone about a mile when the motor died—would you believe we had run out of gas? We flipped coins (odd man out) to see who would take Truitt's small one-gallon gas container and walk to find some gas.

Naturally, with my luck, I lost; so off I strolled, taking along with me an "Oklahoma credit card" (a small, clear plastic hose to siphon gas from some farmer's truck or a highway truck I might find on the highway. Since it was about midnight, I could not just walk up to somebody's door and knock—I might get shot instead. After unsuccessfully trying three or four different houses and being run off by big dogs each time, I gave up trying to get gas that way and just began walking back to Cleburne, with the slim hope of maybe hitching a ride. After about half an hour, lo and behold, I did get a ride from a couple heading back home. They saw me carrying the gas can and felt sorry for me. They dropped me off at the first open gas station we came to, and there was Truitt and the rest of the guys. They had gotten a ride a little bit earlier and were filling up. Truitt then dropped us off at our respective homes, and we thought this chapter in our lives was over.

However, at school, Monday, we five were outside Mr. Wheat's agricultural building at noon, pitching washers with a number of others. Suddenly, I heard someone yelling, and here strode one of the Goatneck guys hollering at Truitt. "Ownby, I recognized your car Friday night! Look at what one of y'all did to my eye!"

Ouch! His right eye was turned about inside out and as purple as a grape. It was the guy my brother had punched. Mr. Goatneck started throwing a fist at Truitt, but he made a serious mistake. Evidently, he did not know that Truitt fought in the Golden Gloves and had done so for five or six years. Plus, he was darn good and fast as lightning. Now he only weighed about 145 pounds (welterweight class), but Goatneck went about 180 to 190, but his size didn't help him. He could not land a single punch on Truitt. In about three minutes flat, Goatneck's face looked like raw hamburger meat, and he was bleeding like a stuck pig. Fortunately for him, Mr. Wheat, hearing the commotion, came running out of his building and stopped the fight. He then marched the two off to Principal Huddelston's office.

To this day, I am so thankful Goatneck had not recognized me or Eldon as the ones sitting in the back seat. I'm confident Eldon could have whupped him, but with me, it would have been a foot race, and fear would have motivated me to run even faster.

# CHAPTER 21

# THE UNWILEY COYOTE AND OTHER ANIMAL TALES

Can one be an animal lover and a Bambi hunter at the same time? I believe one can for I am living evidence of the truth of that statement. I hunted Bambi for about forty years and usually shot one or two nearly every year. I also hunted dove, quail, and duck from time to time. However, I haven't hunted anything in nine or ten years. It just got too expensive for a poor English teacher. I'm also the softhearted type who stops and carries turtles across the road, and rescues spiders from my wife's wrath and safely deposits them outside. My philosophy in hunting was I only shot something that I was going to eat unless it posed a threat to me. For example, I killed a copperhead or two when they were in my garage or yard at my house in Weatherford. Doing so was a must since I had a small son at the time. However, on various deer leases that I have hunted on, I have encountered rattlesnakes from time to time and never killed a single one. They all rattled to warn me they were there; plus, they were there first. Yes, I know I could have shot them and then ate them, but I'm too lazy to go to all the trouble of frying them in batter. And yes, I have eaten "rattler" before at the Sweetwater Round-up, and they do taste like chicken; but you would have to eat about six or seven whole ones to get filled up.

Speaking of snakes, I do not kill them needlessly at any time. About a year ago, I looked out my study window here at our house in Cleburne and saw my wife doing an unusual dance and yelling at the same time. I ran out there, and she had discovered about a four-foot rat snake that had climbed out of our pecan tree. Now she wanted me to kill it, but with its being a harmless and beneficial species, instead I got a Styrofoam chest, scooped the snake into it, and carried it out into the country a ways and released it. Another encounter with a rat snake did not end so successfully.

About seven years ago, we had a Reed reunion down at the city park here in Cleburne. We had reserved the gazebo there just west of the swimming pool. Now this gazebo was surrounded by some sort of bushes that were about six feet tall. When I stepped up on the gazebo, my cousin Johnny from San Angelo greeted me and said there was a large snake in one of the bushes which was frightening the ladies, and they wanted one of the men to kill it and carry it off. I boldly said, "No need to kill it. I'll just catch it and remove it to a safe place."

Johnny said, "Oh, I want to watch this." On various hunting trips and backpacking trips, I had caught snakes in our campsites or campfire areas and carried them off without too much difficulty, so I was confident I could do so again. (What did Robert Burns say about "the best-laid plans"?) Anyway, I walked down the steps and stopped in front of the bush that Johnny indicated. What I planned to do was just grab the snake by the tail, whip it back and forth like a pendulum so it couldn't bite me, and then haul it off a safe distance away. It had worked before, so why not again? I confidently parted the bush with my two hands, and sure enough, there was the snake, nearly at the top of the bush, head up. Grabbing the tail, which was near the ground, would have been no problem. However, pride reared its ugly head. The snake's head was only about six inches from my left hand, and inspiration struck (sort of what had occurred on numerous occasions in my youth)! I could grab the snake right behind the head with my left hand, then grab its tail with my right hand, and walk around showing the snake off to everyone. In theory, it sounded good.

Unfortunately, I am right handed, and my left hand and arm are a little weaker than my right. As I successfully seized the snake right behind its head, it was able to stretch its neck out and latched on to the back of my left hand with its fangs. Now I am hollering and flailing the air with a four-foot snake attached to my left hand. I also am a bleeder since I take Warfarin because of the defibrillator-pacemaker implant that I have. Blood is spurting from my hand, the womenfolk are screaming, and Johnny is dying laughing and turning red in the face. I don't know who I was the maddest at—me, the snake, or Johnny laughing so hard. Fortunately, I shook the snake off, caught him by the tail, as I should have done to start with, did the pendulum bit, and carried him off about a hundred yards and released him. To this day, I have not lived that episode down. I still get ribbed about by my relatives. That pride will do it to us, won't it?

Now to Unwiley Coyote. I have seen coyotes on several of my past deer leases but never shot one. Yes, I know they eat baby deer, quail, etc.; but I respect them as fellow hunters and predators. Therefore, I do not begrudge them an occasional small deer or two. To be exact, I remember on one occasion I went to some lengths to help a coyote in need. About ten or twelve years ago when I was teaching at Tarrant County College—South Campus, Mike, a part-time English teacher there, invited me to go on a shrimping trip with him to Gretna, Louisiana, just the other side of New Orleans. (I will probably write another story sometime about that entire trip for it was indeed memorable.) However, on our drive back home, as we were getting close to Longview, I spotted something unusual. Mike was driving, and while I was staring out my passenger window at all of the trees and pastureland, I saw a coyote hanging from a fence post. Now that is not an unusual sight ordinarily since most ranchers will shoot them and hang them upside down on the post. However, this coyote was hanging head up on the post with its tail touching the ground. That immediately caught my attention, and I yelled at Mike to pull over and stop. He did so. Then I asked him to back up so I could get a better look at this coyote and see what was going on. He backed up to where we were even with the coyote, and we saw the coyote's predicament. He had evidently been trying to leap the fence, coming from the woods side, and one front paw had slipped between the top two strands, flipping him over in a somersault and leaving him hanging there.

I got out of the pickup to get a closer look, to see if it were even alive, and as I did so, the coyote swiveled its head and riveted his eyes on me. His left shoulder and side were covered with blood where he had been thrashing about to free himself, but the twisted strands of barbed wire would not let him. I asked Mike to get me a pair of pliers from his toolbox, and he asked me what I was going to do. I told him, "I'm going to release the coyote."

He asked, "Why do that? It's just a coyote. Besides, what if the rancher comes by and sees you doing that and objects?" I told him I would handle it if that happened, but I did not want to see any animal suffer like that.

He handed me the pliers, and I stepped down into the ditch and approached the coyote. For one of the few times in my life, I actually thought this stunt through before I did it. I noticed, for example, that the coyote was hanging on the highway side of the fence. Now I did not want to cut him loose and we both wind up on the same side of the fence. Therefore, I intelligently climbed over the fence and began cutting the top strand of barbed wire about two feet away from the coyote's head. He was still intently watching me. After

I had severed the strand, I began unwinding it until I reached the coyote's paw, which allowed the coyote to slump, exhausted, to the ground. Seeing that he posed no danger to me, I climbed back over the fence. I then went to the truck, retrieved a plastic bowl from our camping gear, and filled it with water. I carried it back to the coyote and placed it as close to his head as I dared. He still had not moved a muscle. I told him that was all I could do for him, and Mike and I loaded up and drove off.

I will always wonder if he survived the ordeal. I hope so.

# Chapter 22

## Irving Elementary School Memories and Other Educational Experiences

In a previous story entitled "Young Love," I described attending Santa Fe Elementary for five years, but the summer after my fifth-grade year, I learned my platonic love had transferred to Irving

Elementary to attend sixth grade. Being heartbroken, I somehow managed to follow her. (I really did not remember how I finagled that, so for years, I just chalked up my doing so to romantic love. I told this story for about twenty-five years or so until one day, at a Reed gathering, my mother and sister overheard my poignant tale, and Mother quickly interrupted me. "What? You don't remember Santa Fe's vice principal stopping by our house that summer and asking me if I would voluntarily transfer you to Irving because Santa Fe needed a rest?" Well, I certainly did *not* have any memory of that visit—that wasn't romantic at all! Thereafter, when telling my touching first story, I now have to include Mother's rather harsh version too. Oh, well.)

However, I did have other memorable experiences at Irving. A sad one occurred right off when my platonic love quickly took up with one of the football jocks attending there, but time does heal all wounds. Then I encountered a lovely blonde named Ann and actually went on my first official date. My mother drove me to her house where we both got out of the car and walked to the door. (I was relieved that Mom did that for my knees were knocking. Hey, I was only eleven years old!) Ann's mother opened the door; Mom told her she was going to drop us off at the Palace Theater and would have Ann back in three hours. Off we went for an enchanting evening, eating popcorn and watching a movie. (No, I do not remember the movie. Naturally, if it were left up to me, it would have been a Western.) Anyway, we had a lot of fun, but sadly, that was the only date we went on. Evidently, my suave charm must have failed me.

I must have had a fetish for "Anns," for my next best friend was another Ann. She and I shared a unique accomplishment. We absolutely mastered the game of Tic-Tac-Toe or Cat and Rat—whatever title you learned it by. I do not remember how many hours we spent playing that game, but we learned the moves, whereby we could *not* lose. We would tie or be tied, but no one could beat us.

I put my skill at this game to use some fifteen years later when I was teaching British Literature II at Fort Worth Christian College in North Richland Hills in Fort Worth. It was a Friday in my Monday-Wednesday-Friday class. The class met from 9:00 to 9:50 a.m.; I somehow blew through the reading assignment in thirty minutes flat and had twenty minutes to go. I could have started on the next poem, Thomas Hardy's "The Convergence of the Twain," about the sinking of the *Titanic*, but I chose instead to have some fun with the class. Now I did not want to just turn them loose twenty minutes early, so I challenged them. If someone would step to the board and beat me in a game of Tic-Tac-Toe, I would immediately let the whole class go. Instantly, nearly the entire class of twenty or so students lined up to take me on. I then reiterated my challenge—someone had to *beat* me; I won all ties. There were a few objections, but most of them were confident some student could beat me. Fifteen minutes later, I was still standing, undefeated. Since there were now only five minutes left of class time, I did not mind dismissing them, so I did so. However, one male student raised his hand. "Mr. Reed, so you enjoy mind games, mental puzzles?"

I replied, "Somewhat. What do you have in mind?"

He stated, "What if I were to write you out a puzzle, you can work on it the entire weekend; and on Monday, if you do not have the correct answer, you will give the whole class the entire period off. Deal?" I certainly wanted to be fair, and I did not want to be considered a chicken by the class, so I agreed. Boy, the class began cheering as the student wrote down this puzzle and then handed it to me. As I started reading it, recognition struck! I had the answer in a college mathematics textbook that I had at home. However, I kept a poker face and even grimaced and said, "Wow! This is a tough one, but I'll keep my word and give it a try." The class gleefully marched out, confident that Monday was going to be a free period.

Now this math text I had at home was one I had used in this extremely difficult math class I enrolled in during my last semester at North Texas State when I was completing all the course requirements for obtaining my Bachelor of Arts degree in English in May of 1963. I only lacked a few electives to fill out the required 120 hours, and I let a numbskull counselor talk me into taking a fourth math class (I had already taken algebra, trigonometry, and business math, making Cs in the first two and a *B* in the last one). The counselor told me if I took a fourth math class, math would serve as my second minor with twelve hours behind history, my first minor. However, I told him math was my worst subject. I always prayed for a *C* in a math class while in all my other classes, I endeavored to make the highest grade in the class (I knew that was impossible in a math class). He suggested I walk down to the math department anyway and see what courses they had to offer. Like an obedient child, off I went; and sure enough, the man in the office there said he had just the course for me—finite mathematics! I blanched and told him that I knew what a finite <u>verb</u> was, but what in the world was finite mathematics? Then he hooked the male side of me. He said, "Oh, you'll study such things as probabilities—what is the probability of drawing an ace high straight royal flush in poker or rolling snake eyes on a pair of dice? Thus, I dutifully enrolled in this "easy" math class. *Wrong!*

I walked into class that first morning and knew instantly something was fishy here. There were only sixteen students in the class instead of the customary twenty-five or thirty or so. After class, I began asking some questions and discovered that fourteen of the students were *math majors*, the head of the department taught the class, and his last name was Cobb (and he was "as rough as a"). One other idiot and I were enrolled in a special math class, and the other idiot dropped in two weeks when he saw the handwriting on the wall that he was going to flunk. I could not drop, if I did not make at least a *C-* in this class, I would not be walking across the stage in May, graduating with my Bachelor's class. And, boy, are students spoiled today! Grades are seen only by the teacher and the individual student. In that math class, test grades were posted outside, on the classroom door or wall adjacent to the door, listing the student's last name, first initial, and then the numerical grade on the test, in *descending* order, from highest grade to the last. I never had to lift my eyeballs over waist high to see my score: Reed, W—47; Reed, W—41, etc. My name was last on every test! On the final exam, I had to make something like a 150 to pass the class. Now you and I know I could not and did not score a 150, but the grade on my transcript showed a *C-*. God watches over His idiots.

Now back to the student's puzzle that he gave me. It was actually used as an example in that demonic finite mathematics textbook. Here it is: You have been captured by natives. They place you in a hut with two doors; one door leads to freedom, and the other leads to death. There is a guard in front of each door; one always tells the truth, and the other one always lies. You are allowed to ask one question to either of the guards. What question can you ask of either guard, and the answer will guarantee to lead you to the door of freedom?

Here's the answer: ask either guard what door the other guard would say is the exit to freedom and then choose the opposite door. If you ask the guard who always tells the truth, he knows the other guard would lie, so he'll point you to the door leading to death. If you ask the guard who always lies, he knows the other guard would truthfully show you the freedom exit, so he will lie and point you to the door leading to death.

So that following Monday morning, I trudged into class with a glum look on my face, and all the students began to chatter excitedly about getting to skip their dreaded English class. I reluctantly handed my answer on a note card to the student who had given me the brain teaser and told him that was the best answer that I could come up with. He quickly glanced at it and exclaimed, "Oh, no. He got it right!"

The entire class began groaning and moaning, but then I said, "Oh, okay. Y'all can still have the class period off, but your official assignment is go work on your research papers. I'll be in my office if you have any questions regarding it." They all cheered me as they quickly exited the classroom.

So the simple skill of becoming an expert tic-tac-toe player in the sixth grade at Irving Elementary School aided me later on in life while teaching at Fort Worth Christian College. Isn't education wonderful?

# CHAPTER 23

# FUN ON THE FARM

As I was growing up, farm work was pretty much my occupation. I have already described the pleasantries of dairy work (pretty much working from "can see to can't see"). I also recounted my first introduction to the cotton patch and my disastrous effort to speed up the weighing process. However, there were other farm experiences I encountered while endeavoring to earn money while growing up.

Take, for instance, other things I learned while picking cotton, such as the pleasures of chewing tobacco. When I was nine or ten, a neighbor of ours, Mr. Gilles, would sometimes accompany us to the cotton field. There, he would pull out a plug of Days Work or Brown's Mule or Bull of the Woods and bite off a chunk. The first time he offered me some, it made me a little dizzy but not much. In no time flat, I could handle it without too much trouble unless Momma was with us; then I would wait until she was out of sight before I would try some. Brown's Mule and Bull of the Woods were dark plugs and would flat grow hair on your chest. Days Work was easier for me to handle. I do not remember Mr. Gillespie chewing leaf tobacco, like Beechnut or Red Man. Those two I chewed with my neighborhood friends or with my buddy Kenneth out at the Godly dairy.

Another aspect of Mr. Gilles came in "handy" in the cotton patch (pardon the pun), and that was his large hands. Before the term was even used, I'm sure he could "palm" a basketball. When we picked cotton, he would cover two or three rows and still be able to lean over and help me keep up with my one row. Now picking cotton involved just plucking out the white, fluffy fiber with the seed inside and placing that in your cotton sack. Picking season usually began around July and continued sporadically into October. With his large hands and tireless ability, Mr. Gilles was a good picker, able to haul in about five hundred to six hundred pounds a day. At my age, I was lucky to gather in a hundred. His large hands really aided him when we pulled cotton. In "pulling bolls," as it was called, the worker would place a hand at the base of the cotton stalk, palm up, and simply slide it up the stalk, taking everything with it—cotton boll, leaves, and all. Thus, Mr. Gilles excelled at this task while I did not fare as well with my little hands. Pulling bolls occurred for a late-blooming crop or poor crops due to drought or too much rain.

Another truly fascinating farm job was threshing oats. Wouldn't you know it? My Uncle O. B. introduced me to this fun occupation. During several summers, he would take me with him in his truck that had a bed with wooden sideboards for hauling various loads, this time being, oat sheaves. I don't quite remember with confidence what he paid me for a day's work, something like two or three dollars for some pretty backbreaking work. He would drive out into the oat fields, which contained row upon row of oat shocks (teepee shaped) stacked and ready for us guys on the ground to attack with our pitchforks. A machine called a binder had already come along and cut and tied the oat stalks into bundles or sheaves. Then other workers had stacked them up in a teepee fashion with nine or ten sheaves per shock. Uncle O. B. would drive up beside a shock, and a couple of other workers and I would stab one side of the shock and start tossing the sheaves impaled on our forks over into the back of his truck. When the back of his truck was full, he would drive over to the nearby thresher where other workers would toss his load into the machine, which separated the seeds from the stalks. Then the seeds were blown into an adjacent grain silo. We did this every day until that job was finished for that particular farmer. Oh, what fun! My older brother Eldon, who had graduated the previous year and was living in Dallas, came out one Saturday and worked with us, but he never returned. Imagine that!

There were several other farm tasks that I was fortunate enough to experience. Let me tell you that hauling hay was fun, fun, fun! I was paid ten cents a bale to help move the hay from the field to the barn. I usually was a loader, walking along beside the trailer or truck and lifting the bale and tossing it on the bed to be stacked by the person handling that chore. Sometimes, I would be the stacker on the trailer; however, I did not want to be the stacker in the barn. Man, that was a tough job, having to handle every bale and stack them up to the roof! Not a pleasant way to earn money. Digging postholes wasn't so easy either and certainly not at ten cents a hole. Fortunately, older guys usually tamped the poles in, stretched the wire, and hung the gates.

One final job I had in my senior year at Cleburne High did not involve farm work and was literally what hunting folks would call "a bird nest on the ground," in other words, easy pickings. I landed a position working at the Dairy Queen on North Main. I had the pleasure of being interviewed and hired by the owner. What a cushy job! Get this—air-conditioned! Wow! No working out in the hot sun, no blisters on the hands, no aching back! Another amenity was they fed us every shift—we got the choice of either a hamburger or a barbeque sandwich. Now I would pull something sneaky here. The hamburger bun was larger than the barbeque bun, so I would grab the larger one and load it up with barbeque. Plus, another added attraction involved the chocolate dipped cone. If when dipping the cone in the chocolate syrup, if the ice cream happened to drop down into the syrup bowl, we could ladle that aside and eat it on our break. Man, I perfected the method of knowing just how far not to press the ice cream to guarantee that it would drop off every time.

Yes, sir, I really loved that city-slicker job. The farming experiences I could have done without.

# CHAPTER 24

# MY CAT MOUSEY

I introduced Mousey to you in an earlier story about my dad and the antipathy that he felt toward most animals in general. He did make an exception in Mousey's case because she was death to mice and a terror to our neighborhood dogs. However, Mousey was special to me, really more like my second sister.

For one thing, she always slept with me—if she did not have a litter of kittens. She did have a bunch of them, by the way. My sister kept track of the number and said that in her fourteen years, Mousey had ninety-nine kittens in total. There certainly was no shortage of cats on the northeast side of Cleburne. Now there was no telling where Mousey would give birth to her litter. Mother always had an apple crate in a corner of the closet, complete with an old towel or blanket and in a secluded, private spot. However, one of us kids would pull open our drawer to get a pair of underwear some morning, and there Mousey would be, purring contentedly with four or five kittens, nursing away.

On some occasions, Mousey would be swollen the previous day and then show up the next morning at the back door, slim as could be. It was then my job to follow her and see where she had had her litter. Sometimes, it would only be a short trip to our storage shed out back, where I would retrieve the kittens and take them into the house, with Mousey following me, plaintively meowing with great concern. I would dutifully put them in the apple crate in the closet; sometimes Mousey would relent and leave them there. Other times, she would move them again; and once again, I would have to play detective to find them.

Now and then, I would have to follow her into the Santa Fe shops. There, sleuthing really was required to not lose track of her. Usually, she would have the litter under a stack of railroad rails or crossties. Then I would have to crawl underneath the stack, retrieve the four or five kittens, and make my way home, again with Mousey following me quite nervously.

However, during those intervals when she had no kittens and I would hit the sack, here would come Mousey. In the warm months, she would sleep at my feet, where she demanded that I be as still as possible. If I dared to move my feet and disturb her, a sharp bite on one of the offending appendages would ensure my complete cooperation. On cold nights, when I would have my blankets pulled up around my shoulders, first I would feel her jump up on my bed near my face. Then she would begin pawing at the blankets, demanding entrance. Naturally, I never hesitated to lift up the covers and let her in, where she would crawl down to the foot of the bed. Again, I was to keep my feet still or else. I endured that because, after all, she was my buddy, and I loved her dearly.

Then one day, I had to make a tough decision. It was the last weekend in August after I had just graduated from high school. I had also recently married my high-school sweetheart, and she and I were moving to Abilene that weekend to begin attending Abilene Christian College. I was the only family member living at home for my mom was living in Dallas to be close to and attend to my dad, who had been in a horrendous car wreck in February and was in the V. A. hospital in Dallas. Our house on Sabine was going to be empty for months, and I could not take Mousey with me to live in a thirty-foot trailer house with my wife and me. Thus, I had to find another home for her. Some former next-door neighbors, Mose and Sue, had moved out in the country on the Covington road and could use a good cat to handle the mice and rats out there. So on Friday of that last weekend in August, I took Mousey and her apple crate bed that she sometimes napped in, and we drove out to Mose and Sue's in a car I had borrowed from my Uncle O. B. (I did not have a car of my own). Of course, Mousey did not like the car ride (I guess thinking she was going to the vet), nor did she care for Mose and Sue's house when I took her inside. I stressed to them that they had to keep Mousey inside the house for at least a week because a cat ordinarily attaches itself to the house and not really to the occupants. The house owners, the cat just tolerates. I was hoping that one week would be long enough for Mousey to acclimate herself to their house and settle in. Having to leave her, my second sister and best friend, was heart rending, but taking her with me to Abilene seemed to be out of the question. Therefore, off I drove, heavy of heart, dropped off Uncle O. B.'s car, and Linda and her parents picked me up with the little house trailer in tow as we headed to Abilene.

After setting up the trailer at the site awaiting it at the end of the married couples' dorm on ACC's campus, Linda's parents left. She and I took a tour of the campus and began to acquaint ourselves with college life. Everything was going great for a couple of days until Sunday afternoon, the married couples' dorm supervisor knocked on our door and told me I had a phone call for me on the payphone in the lobby. My heart sank when I heard Sue's voice, and she told me Mousey had slipped out of their house and had disappeared. She apologized profusely, and I told her it was all right, and I would be back in Cleburne on Monday to look for her. That Monday, I took a Greyhound bus from Abilene to the station in Cleburne with Uncle O. B. meeting me there and letting me borrow his car again after I dropped him off. I spent the next two days hiking all over the countryside around Mose and Sue's house, frantically searching for Mousey and calling for her but had no luck. Need I mention that I bawled like a baby? I blamed myself, naturally, for literally abandoning my best friend, and it was another gloomy bus ride back to Abilene on Thursday morning.

Of course, my wife Linda was awaiting me and hugged me, offering comfort for my loss. In addition, there was something else at the trailer house that gave me the opportunity to take my mind off losing Mousey somewhat. Our little house sat on an alley, and when we had arrived the previous week, there were about fifteen to twenty cats roaming all over the place. After purchasing some cat food from a nearby store, I commenced to make friends with my new feline acquaintances and began to give some of them names, like Jack and Jill, Blacky, Patches, Shadow, etc. Being around them assuaged my grief a little until something occurred after one semester. In the fall, I had taken biology; and then in the spring, I signed up for zoology. In the lab for this class, trouble started. At first, we had cut up earthworms, then frogs (boy, what a waste of good frog legs), and lastly, piglets. I had no problem carrying out the required assignments of cutting those critters asunder. However, after we had finished the study of the pigs, our lab instructor told us that we would begin a new project the next class period.

I walked into the lab two days later and nearly fainted, plus came very close to vomiting. There, stretched out at every station, were cats to be carved up. And not just any old cats, but my friends from the alley! Some college guys had captured about fifteen of them and sold them to the zoology lab folk. As I stood there dumbfounded, my lab teacher told me, "Weldon, don't just stand there. Get to your station and commence to cutting."

My first inclination was to punch him, but fortunately, I restrained myself. Through clenched teeth, I told him there was no way I was about to cut on a cat. First of all, I was a devout cat lover, and furthermore, I knew about every one of those cats, and I was not going to touch a single one of them.

He replied, "Well, I'll have to give you an *F* on the assignment."

I said, "Let's go talk to the department chair," and off we went. At the chair's office, I told him about my cat Mousey, my best friend for fourteen years, and how I could not bring myself to cut on a cat. Instead, I told him to bring a cadaver to class; I would much prefer to cut on a human corpse than on a cat. Evidently, my department chair must have been a cat lover too for he told the lab instructor to let me work on another pig.

You know, I still miss that old cat, and I hope she merely ran off to somebody else's house out there in the country and got fat on those country mice.

# CHAPTER 25

# MORE ILLEGAL WAYS TO FISH

I have already introduced my dad's skill with grabbling, catching fish by hand, feeling underneath large rocks in a river or in holes underneath the bank. Naturally, game wardens tended to frown on such activities, as my dad and I nearly discovered one time, but Dad's quick thinking saved us from being arrested. (Okay, the warden would probably only have arrested Dad, but remember, I had already been arrested at the age of twelve for stealing a mere thirty-five-cent wheel bearing for my bicycle. They probably would have hung me for grabbling.)

I was about fourteen at this time when Dad and I were wading down this creek on a friend Joe's property near Weatherford. We had caught about six or seven fish, but Mose, our neighbor, was not there with us with his tow sack to collect the fish. He probably was still holding a grudge about Dad throwing that snake at him. Anyway, I was carrying a metal fish stringer and hooking the fish on it while Dad did most of the grabbling. Suddenly, Dad said, "Son, submerge that stringer, stand on it, and then splash around like you're playing in the water."

I said, "Why? What's the matter?"

He said, "Here comes a game warden." Sure enough, I looked across this meadow, and here came a man in a green uniform. He walked up to the creek's edge and said howdy to us. Dad said "Howdy" back, and the warden then asked him what we were doing. Dad said he was just taking me swimming. Meanwhile, I was merrily splashing around in the water, sometimes putting my head under and coming up sputtering. The warden looked up and down the creek, and then bid us goodbye. Close call, right?

Another slightly illegal method of catching fish that Daddy sometimes employed was telephoning. Evidently, this was a far worse offense than grabbling because he never took me with him when he engaged in this activity. He would just tell me about it when he got back and showed us the fish he had "caught." In telephoning, you would use one of the old crank-handled wall phones. You would then connect two bare wires, about twenty feet long each, to the electrodes on the magnet inside and drop them over each side of the boat. Then you would start cranking the handle as you troll around. A fish touching one of the wires would be temporarily stunned and float to the top of the water for the hardworking fisherman to pick up in a dip net. For some reason, this method of fishing primarily affected catfish; scaled fish seemed immune to the stunning. However, nothing beats eating fresh catfish anyway to us ol' country boys. Now if you were caught by a game warden, I suppose you could always tell them you were cranking up some ice cream.

A final illegal method that Dad would use was rotenone, a crystalline substance used in insecticides, available in farming or agricultural stores. I have heard that ground-up walnuts would work too, but Dad always used rotenone. He would buy a pound or two of the product, and we would drive to a stock tank near Cleburne. He would then put the rotenone in a tow sack, along with a heavy rock. He or I would then wade around in this tank, dragging the tow sack behind us in the water. This method only worked in a small body of water that was totally enclosed and had no free-flowing outlet. We would then sit on the bank for about five or ten minutes until, magically, any scaled fish in the water would float to the top of the water, saying, "Weldon, pick me up, pick me up." For some reason, this did not seem to bother catfish. The rotenone would, evidently, inhibit the breathing of the scaled fish momentarily. However, the drug had no effect on humans for we always ate the fish with no problems.

Fish was usually a weekly staple of the Reed family's menu, and I certainly never objected to it. Plus, catching the fish always involved an air of adventure.

# CHAPTER 26

# MY GRIDIRON PROWESS (OR LACK THEREOF)

I was introduced to football in the sixth grade at Irving Elementary School. My memory could be a tad hazy here, but as best as I can remember, a bunch of us guys signed up and gathered after school in the evenings to practice that fall. I recollect we would load up in a bus and drive to Yellow Jacket Stadium where we trooped beneath the stands into this old locker room. We then put on these ratty uniforms which had seen some wear and tear. I had to watch the other kids to learn where to slip the plastic pads into the front of the pants to protect my legs. The shoulder pads and helmets, I could pretty well figure out. Then we went outside onto the field. Naturally, being somewhat on the small side, I had no chance at making the first team or even the second for that matter. I was just an extra, you might say. (Weighing only a sizzling seventy pounds, what did I expect?) However, I do remember playing a little at left cornerback and sometimes at left linebacker. Man, I loved the action, the banging into the line, trying to bring down the runner. Of course, I usually got run over and flattened; but, hey, it was fun. I absolutely loved the game. However, remember what the Good Book says, "The spirit is willing, but the flesh is weak." Boy, my spirit loved to play, but my scrawny body did not have enough weight to really make an impact.

I do not recollect how many other elementary schools we played, and I am sure that we had to have a permission form signed by one of our parents. Now I know my mother would not have signed one for her baby boy to get beat up and knocked around. So who signed that letter? I could not have done it myself; my handwriting has always resembled something written by a broken-legged chicken. I checked with my sister Melba recently, and she proclaimed her innocence, stating she would not have dared go against Momma like that. Since my Uncle O. B. is no longer around to proclaim differently, I'll just blame (or thank) him. Anyway, I got to play that year a little and loved it. I checked with my football buddy and stud player Pat to confirm some of these facts, and he informed me that Irving won the city championship that year against Adams Elementary. Certainly, Pat played a major role in that, along with Wayne, James, Timmy, Rex, and others. Looking back, I wistfully wish I could have borrowed some height and weight from those guys. Just think—I might have been a stud like them. Oh, well, if wishes were horses.

Next, I attempted to continue my football accomplishments at dear ol' Fulton Junior High. We had football practice in the spring, preparing for the fall games. I do remember that our coach ran a tight ship, and he certainly had the respect (fear, actually) of all the guys. He was a large man, red headed, and you did not want to get on his bad side. I was in his history class as well, and if some knucklehead on the back row acted up, Coach would brain that person with an eraser while still sitting in his chair. He was just that stern on the football field. Again, I did not even make the second team, so I was just an extra, a body to put in there to fill up a space. From time to time, I would go in at left cornerback or left linebacker. However, sometimes, Coach would put me in at fullback. Wow, what an impression—a seventy-five or eighty-pound beast lining up behind the quarterback! The halfback behind me outweighed me twenty pounds or so, but I always endeavored to give it my best shot.

I'll never forget what occurred one evening. Coach had sent me in at fullback, and I was snorting fire as I approached the huddle, determined to slam into that line, creating a mammoth hole for the halfback. To my surprise (to my shock, really), Robert, the quarterback, called "fullback dive" on the first play. This was a play where the quarterback, under center, just takes the snap, turns around, and sets the ball in my arms as I come flying past him. I could see myself smashing through the line, flattening cornerbacks and safeties, running free for a touchdown. However, my fantasy did not quite come to fruition. As I shot forward when Robert took the snap, he, instead of firmly setting the ball in my spread arms, slammed the ball into my stomach, totally knocking the breath out of me, and I fell gasping, flat on my face on the ground. Naturally, the entire team died laughing, as did Coach. Something tells me that this was a joke set up by that quarterback. Oh, well, I gave all of the guys something to laugh about for days, but something far sadder occurred after spring training was over. My mother would not sign the permission slip for me to play in actual games in the fall. I pleaded, begged, cajoled, but to no avail. Man, was I crushed! A possible Dick Butkus career nipped in the bud.

When eighth grade rolled around, I again pleaded with my mother to let me come out for spring training. She reluctantly agreed, warning me that I had better not come home with a broken bone or blood on me. I was ecstatic, another chance to play the game I loved. This year was pretty much like the previous, my being sent in now and then just to fill a position for a few plays. I would always give 110 percent though, striving mightily to make a good play. Then the time rolled around for us to get our parents' signature on the permission form. Again, my mother was pretty adamant about not signing it. Again, I pleaded, begged, cajoled; but Momma was standing pretty firm. Finally, I suggested something to her. "Momma, come down tomorrow and watch our last scrimmage. Then you'll see that nobody ever gets hurt. Shoot, we're all wearing all that equipment. We just knock each other around and get right up." Reluctantly, she agreed, and I was euphoric! This year, I would be able to actually play in a game, maybe scoring a touchdown or recovering a fumble, being carried off the field on my teammates' shoulders.

The next day dawned, and I was excitedly awaiting our scrimmage that evening. School finally let out, and I got dressed for practice in record speed. About twenty minutes after we started, I saw Momma drive up and park close to the fence where she had a good view. As usual, I did not get put in until toward the end of the scrimmage, but here I entered to play left linebacker. As luck would have it, the first play called by the offense was a sweep to the left side. I think Rex was playing that side, and he slid over to do his job, break up the wedge in front of the halfback. My job, along with the cornerback on that side and the safety, was to tackle the runner. I believe Rex must have led with his mouth as he slammed into the blockers. The cornerback made the tackle, and then everyone got up from the pile. Immediately, everybody saw what had happened. Rex's upper lip was split wide open with blood and gore pouring down the front of his white jersey.

My mother, upon seeing that gruesome sight, began yelling as loud as she could. "Weldon Thomas, Weldon Thomas, get off that field right now!" My shame, my humiliation, was more than I could stand. Of course, all the guys were laughing again at my expense, and little Mommy's boy slunk to the car. It was not a pleasant experience.

# CHAPTER 27

## CLOSE ENCOUNTERS OF THE ANIMAL KIND

Anumber of curious events occurred in my life from time to time. In and of themselves, they were short interludes that entertained me, amused me, instructed me, or taught me a much-needed lesson or two, which I usually ignored and went on to commit various other zany stunts. Some of these events involved animals.

One interesting episode began one night when Dad arrived home from fishing with some friends (yes, somewhat illegal fishing again—this time, with a seine or net, which game wardens did frown on). In addition to some catfish, bass, croppie, and sand bass, Dad's catch also included the largest frog I had ever seen. Its body was larger than a dinner plate, and I swear it had to weigh about ten pounds. Ordinarily, with frogs, Dad would go ahead and kill it, cutting off its rear legs for Momma to fry. Frog legs were pretty much a staple part of our diet as were fish, rabbit, and squirrel. However, instead of killing the frog as soon as he got home, Dad wanted to keep it overnight and show it off to his friends at the Santa Fe shops. Thus, he and I went outside where Dad placed a No. 3 washtub on the ground, threw the frog underneath it, and then placed about a twenty- pound rock on top of it to secure the frog.

Unfortunately, the next morning when Dad and I went to retrieve the frog, the tub was turned over, and Froggy was gone. Boy, was Dad mad! He could not believe that frog had literally hopped out from under that tub. Naturally, we searched all around the house, shed, and chicken pen but no frog. Dad went to work in a foul mood, to say the least. Three days later, while Dad was eating breakfast before he went to work, he opened up the Cleburne paper and suddenly yelled out loud, "He killed my frog!" There on the front page was a picture of a man with a shotgun in one hand and in the other, he was holding Dad's frog. The headline read: "Giant Frog Attacks Santa Fe Railroad Night Watchman!" The man told a reporter that two nights ago, he had been sitting in his chair underneath this light post when he saw a large shape hopping out of the dark, straight toward him. In self-defense, he aimed his shotgun and fired at his approaching assailant, which turned out to be our escaped meal. His guard post was located about two hundred and fifty yards from our house; our property on Sabine Street butted up against the wooden fence belonging to the Santa Fe railroad. Darn, that frog's large rear legs would have tasted great!

Another animal experience of mine involved a unique crow. When I was about thirteen or fourteen, Dad and I were headed to Lake Whitney to go fishing, and we stopped off in Rio Vista at their local bait shop to pick up some minnows. While Dad was with the owner getting the minnows, I was just wandering around the aisles, looking at the fishing rods, stringers, bobbers, and such when I spotted a large gold birdcage sitting on a shelf. Inside the cage was a cotton-pickin' crow. Now it's not every day that you see someone with a pet crow in a cage. Naturally, I stopped at the birdcage and began looking the crow over. At the same time, he was looking me over pretty good, cocking his head from one side to the other and eyeing me somewhat suspiciously, I thought. Well, you can only stare at a crow just so long, I suppose, and my interest had waned, so I started walking away. Suddenly, that crow squawked an intelligible sentence at me, which made me jump about a foot in the air and two feet backward to get away from him. I'm serious—that crow talked! It uttered this statement at me just as clear as a bell: "I want my bottle!" If I'm lyin', I'm dyin'! I promise you that was exactly what that bird said, and at that age, I certainly had not read Edgar Allan Poe's "The Raven" yet, so that poem had not influenced me. Dad heard it too, for he jerked around, looked at the crow, and asked the bait shop owner, "What did that bird say?"

The owner said, "You heard him right—'I want my bottle.'"

Dad then asked the man where he got that bird, and the owner explained that a guy had stopped in about a week back, needing gas but had no money, but he did say he had a talking crow. He demonstrated the bird's ability to the bait shop owner, who then offered to give the guy a fill-up in exchange for the crow. Off the fellow drove with a full tank of gas, and the shop owner possessed the most unique bird I have every encountered.

A final interlude involving an animal took place shortly after the crow incident. Some buddies and I were walking downtown from our houses on Sabine, and the route we chose this time was to follow Boone over to North Main and then south to downtown. As we approached the KCLE building, we noticed a large crowd had gathered in front and on the side of the radio station. Well, naturally, we had to see what all the commotion was about, so we ambled across the street and slipped through the crowd up to the front row. Some sort of promotion was going on, and would you believe it? There was a trained bear on a chain with leather pads on his paws and a leather muzzle on as well. Some man out in front had a microphone in his hand, and he asked for a volunteer to step forward who wanted to wrestle this bear. I'm looking at this bear and thinking who would be stupid enough to wrestle that big thing. It looked like it weighed about three hundred pounds. Suddenly, a stupid volunteer appeared. One of my buddies pushed me from the back, and I staggered forward! The announcer excitedly shouted, "Ladies and gentlemen, we have a volunteer! Come here, young man. What is your name?" I mumbled my name to him, desiring only to chase my former friend down and put a knot on his head.

The bear's trainer motioned me forward, to approach the bear, so what could I do? I wasn't going to turn tail and run, not in front of my friends and this crowd of people, so I stepped forward and put my arms out like I had seen the wrestlers do on television (you know, those professionals then like Cyclone Anaya, Killer Kowalski, Bull Curry, Gorgeous George, the good ol' days). Well, this fearsome wrestling match did not last too long. The bear mildly shuffled up to me, put his arms around me in a real "bear hug," and gently leaned forward, pushing me over backward with him on top of me, squashing my very breath out of me. Naturally, my friends were dying laughing, the crowd was dying laughing, the announcer was dying laughing. I was merely dying.

But hey, how many people do you know who have actually wrestled a bear? Now you know one.

# CHAPTER 28

# THE TWO BIGGEST EVENTS IN JOHNSON COUNTY

How many young teenaged boys dreamed of running off and joining the circus or a carnival? For me, it was a carnival. I did not see a genuine circus until I was married and had children of my own, but as a kid, I visited a carnival twice a year at the two main entertainment events that occurred in Cleburne: the Johnson County Pioneer and Old Settlers Reunion (we just called it the Alvarado Reunion), and the Johnson County Sheriff's Posse Rodeo.

The rodeo, I believe, rolled around every June, and the ensuing parade and performances were greatly anticipated. These magnificent horses and riders clip-clopped their way through the downtown streets and out to the fairgrounds just west of town, where the rodeo was held back then and the adjacent Midway was set up. As I stood in the crowd and watched those beautiful horses trot by, I would pick out the one I wanted: a palomino like Roy Roger's Trigger or a white one like Silver, the Lone Ranger's horse, maybe a coal black one like in Walter Farley's novel or a beautiful black-and-white paint like the Cisco Kid's Diablo or Gene Autry's famous chestnut, Champion. (Hey, a young boy can dream, can't he?)

Now when actually attending the rodeo itself, I no longer dreamed. I did not envision myself becoming a rodeo star. There was no way I ever wanted to try bulldogging a steer or saddle or bronc riding. Definitely, I did not want to get on the back of a Brahma bull. However, the rodeo itself held another attraction for me and some of my nefarious friends. We used the rodeo to raise money in a slightly illegal way. Imagine that. I do not remember which one of us came up with this money-making scheme, whether it was Ronnie, Carol, Jackie, or whoever; but it did work. Instead of buying a ticket at the front gate, we would slip around way to the back of the arena itself, back where the holding pens were for all of the livestock. There we would crawl under the fence and nonchalantly stroll down the front aisle that led to the entrance gate. Now at the time, there was no restroom inside the rodeo arena itself. You had to get a restroom pass from the ticket taker, which was a ticket stub for the event itself. After visiting the restroom nearby, you came back to the front gate, handed the man your ticket stub, and he would let you back into the rodeo. However, instead of returning to the gate, we would hang around the gate and look for people about to buy a ticket to go inside. I believe the tickets cost around two dollars and fifty cents apiece. We would sell our stub for one dollar, and then we would stroll around to the back fence and repeat the procedure. We might change shirts or ball caps so we would look different. But with two or three dollars now in our pockets, we could roam the Midway, flirt with the girls, and ride some of the rides or visit some of the booths.

However, when it came to enjoying the Midway, the Alvarado Reunion was the cream of the crop to me. First, it seemed to have all the rides in the world there, some of which I liked and some I didn't. Those swinging chairs, the ones that nearly swung you horizontal, I really didn't care for. I tried them a couple of times, usually on a dare, but I always had a little bit of a queasy stomach; and I guarantee you I upchucked both times, which really did not please the crowd gathered around the fence (oops, sorry). Even the Tilt-A-Whirl would bother me a little bit, but I would endure it in order to sit close to the girls my friends and I would be with (or whom we had met that night). Now the Ferris wheel and the merry-go-round were fine, doubly so if you're sitting next to a girl. We enjoyed the bumper cars and the small roller coasters; of course, on the latter, we always had to hold our arms up and not hold on to show how brave we were.

Then we would spend some time visiting some of the booths. If my parents were with me, my favorite booths were where you chunked baseballs to knock over stuffed dolls or the wooden milk bottles. I especially enjoyed these because Dad would always win a stuffed toy or two, and then the barker at the booth would not let him play anymore; or if he recognized Dad from last year, the man would not let Dad play at all. (I've mentioned in a prior story that Dad used to pitch in a semi-pro league. Unfortunately, I did not inherit his ability.) Now chunking the darts at the balloons, I could handle okay or tossing the rings over the bottle tops. Also, Dad and I always enjoyed the shooting gallery; he was pretty good at that too since he hunted quite a bit.

However, the sideshows always were fascinating. Yes, we would pay a quarter to see the fat lady, the sword swallower, or the snake charmer. (Hey, that python was huge! I always wondered if Dad would try to pull that sucker out from under a rock in the Brazos River.) Now the bearded lady did not appeal to me too much, nor the pincushion guy that looked like it would really hurt. Also, the two-headed calf was rather sad. But I remember one sideshow that my brother and I visited that really made an impression on me. It must have, because I still today can remember just about the entire spiel that the barker uttered: "Come see her, folks. She's live, she's real—the Louisiana Swamp Girl! Watch her kill a chicken, pluck the feathers off, tear the chicken apart, and then rip the meat from the bones like a vicious animal!" Man, that was something I had to see. I was with my brother at the time, and we slapped a quarter down apiece and entered the tent to see this wild woman from the swamps. We walked up this elevated ramp which encircled this pen, and thus, we were looking down at this creature. Now the barker had used the term "girl"—let me assure you this woman had not been a girl for thirty or forty years. The word "hag" would more accurately describe her. She was squatting there in the middle of this pen, and sure enough, there were a half dozen chickens running around her.

The barker closed the entrance door and nodded to the Swamp Woman, who then quickly reached out and grabbed a passing chicken by the leg. Amidst much squawking, the hag then changed her grip to the chicken's neck, began revving it up (wringing its neck, to you neophytes), and then held up just the head of the poor chicken, which was now flopping around the pen. Naturally, all the girls around the wall of the ramp were screaming and hiding their eyes. We boys were actually laughing. Then the hag began plucking the chicken, revealing its bare belly and legs, and started pulling the chicken apart. Now I must admit, when she grabbed a handful of entrails and then reared back as if to throw them at everybody, I ducked just like everybody else. Then, folks, I kid you not—she began chomping on that raw, bloody leg as if she were starving to death. At that moment, everybody began filing (some running) toward the door. I told my brother as we were leaving, "Man, whatever they are paying her, it's not enough!"

Those were some unforgettable memories. Several years ago, feeling nostalgic, I revisited the Alvarado Reunion, and, darn, it was not as huge as I remembered it. Even worse, I looked and looked but never found the sideshow advertising, "The Louisiana Swamp Girl." What a disappointment!

# CHAPTER 29

# STAR-CROSSED LOVERS—PART I (LOVE'S LABOR NOT LOST)

Do you believe in love at first sight? I know, I know—fairy tales and movies, right? Tom Hanks in *Sleepless in Seattle* sees Meg Ryan for the first time at the airport. (Okay, so I'm a hopeless romantic. I love that movie and watch it every time it comes on as well as *You Got Mail!*) It happened to Tom Sawyer too when he first saw Becky

Thatcher (a good parallel to the story I am about to tell you—the seemingly unattainable angel). A more modern example of love at first sight is Peeta in *Hunger Games*, who falls in love with Katnis when he was *five*. Now that is "young love"!

Let me begin *my* fairy tale. It occurred when I was a junior in high school at dear ol' Cleburne High. Rex (yes, my buddy from junior high) and I were sitting in Ms. Hooper's English class on the first day of school when "she" walked in the door and stood there for just a moment, evidently looking for an empty desk, but that moment was all it took for me to be totally smitten. Rex and I both nudged each other at the same time and whispered, "Who is that?" She was a new girl in school, and by that afternoon, we had discovered her name and a little background about her. Her name was Linda (I will withhold the last name for privacy's sake), and she and her parents had moved to Cleburne from Fort Worth over the summer. Her father was in construction, building houses, and he had just completed their own two-and-a-half story brick house on the outskirts of Cleburne on Highway 4 east of the cemetery a couple of miles.

Rex and I immediately began double-dog daring one another to ask her for a date. There was just no way I was going to; I just did not have the nerve. Come on. I was literally "the poor boy across the tracks." Her parents were rather well off, shall we say. She lived in a brick house; I had never even been inside one before. Plus, I lived in a four-room frame house, and we still had just an "outhouse"—but hey, it was a two-holer! I thought that was pretty fancy. Anyway, you can see my dilemma. Linda was totally out of my league, untouchable and unattainable, until the unthinkable occurred. A couple of months after school had started, Rex came into Ms. Hooper's class one Monday morning, grinning from ear to ear. "Guess where I went Friday night," he asked.

"Okay, I give up," I replied. "Where?"

He answered, "I took Linda to the Esquire Theatre."

"You didn't!" I exclaimed.

"Sure did," he responded, and then he briefly told how it went and how it ended, that he did not have nerve enough to try for a goodnight kiss.

Boy, I was reeling now. She went on a date with Rex? Well, if she would accept a date with him, maybe I had a chance too. Therefore, I passed the rest of the day, trying to catch her alone so no one else would see her turn me down flat. Sure enough, as school let out, I saw her ahead of me, walking down the front steps with no one close to her. With my heart pounding, I stepped up beside her and said, "Hi, Linda, would you want to go to the movies with me this coming Friday?"

"Sure," she responded. "Pick me up at seven?"

"I'll be there with bells on," I replied. Trust me; I did not *walk* away; I floated on air. On the drive to her house Friday night, I was both euphoric and frightened at the same time. As I pulled up the driveway to her impressive house, my insecurities again began rising. "What am I doing?" I asked myself. Oh, well, nothing ventured, nothing gained. I bravely walked up the sidewalk and rang her front doorbell. She answered pretty promptly and invited me inside to meet her parents, which I could have done without but knew that it was inevitable. I said hello to her very sweet mother, shook hands with her father (who eyed me very suspiciously), and then we escaped to my parents' car. What a relief to have that over with!

On the drive to the Esquire Theatre, the classiest theater in town, I commented to Linda how pretty the dress was that she was wearing. It was a deep-blue, form-fitting one made out of some soft, felt-like fabric. As we parked across the street from the theater, with the passenger side against the curb, I got out, walked around, and opened her door. I then helped her out, we walked around to the front of the car, and I gave her my hand to aid her in stepping off the curb (a rather high one). As she stepped down off it, we heard a ripping sound—that form-fitting dress had ripped from her knee to her upper thigh. I nearly fainted! I'm going to have to take her home with a torn dress on our first date! Plus, her father was an avid hunter; his living room had mounted deer and caribou heads everywhere. I could picture him chasing me out the front door with his shotgun in his hand! Linda calmed me down and said she still wanted to see the movie; all I had to do was walk beside her, holding the torn strip together with one hand. She said the movies would be dark and no one would be able to see. When we left, I would repeat the process, and she would explain what had happened to her parents. I would not even have to come inside if I were so worried. Wow, what a relief! I could not even tell you what the movie was about; my mind was in such a whirl. After the typical movie, popcorn, and drinks, I drove her home, walked her to her door, told her I had a good time, and beat a hasty retreat before the father and shotgun appeared.

Lo and behold, the next Monday morning as I was walking to second period English class, somebody nudged me from behind, and Linda walked up beside me, smiling. That gave me the nerve to ask her out again and, miracle of miracles, she said yes. From that moment on, we started dating once a week somewhere, like the skating rink or putt-putt golf down at the city park. In addition, she was not dating anyone else, and neither was I. By the time January rolled around, I was getting serious enough that I asked her to "go steady"; she wanted to, but her father refused that arrangement. I was hurt and issued an ultimatum—go steady or we wouldn't date at all. Her father won out, and I withdrew into my shell (you know how stubborn and selfish we guys can get. I did not want to share her with anyone). Life went on the rest of that spring semester. I survived. I was elected cheerleader for Edison House, which was not my idea. Some of my friends did not like the one other guy who was running. The idea of free attendance to all the football games, plus one of the sweetest girls in the world as my partner from Adams House persuaded me. (Plus, Sandra was the best tennis player at Cleburne. I loved challenging her but never came close to beating her.) I did not date anyone else until the junior-senior prom. Then I heard that Linda was going to be escorted by this other guy whom she had been dating in Fort Worth before she moved down here. That motivated me to attend with someone else too, which I did. However, I just turned green whenever I would glance Linda's way and see her with her date. It was not a pleasant evening.

Our tumultuous junior year ended, and I was busy then with working in the cotton patch, threshing oats with my Uncle O. B., and sulking, thinking about Linda. Then toward the middle of June, she called me to ask if I would meet her down at the tennis courts at the city park to teach her how to play tennis. She had a cousin coming up from Corpus Christi, and she wanted to be able to play a little with him. Reluctantly, I agreed, realizing that this would just be pouring salt on my open wound (my split-open heart); but I guess I was a glutton for punishment, so I agreed and drove to meet her at the appointed time. When I arrived down at the park, I just about exploded. Linda was there, all right, but she was with one of the high school guys who did not rank too high on my totem pole. To be exact, he was one of the bunch from my Fulton Junior High home-room that Rex and I had tangled with on that memorable occasion. What a wonderful time I was going to have teaching her tennis now, right? Oh, well, I went through with it, worked with her for about forty-five minutes with What's-His-Face leering at me as he sat in his car parked at the fence. Then I told her I had some work to do and left. I should have known better, but it seems I always had to learn my lessons the hard way.

(To be continued. This is a long story)

# CHAPTER 30

## STAR-CROSSED LOVERS—PART II

D o you remember the 1955 song by the Four Aces entitled "Love Is a Many Splendored Thing"? That title only applies to a love affair that is going beautifully and ends in a "happy ever after" marriage, right? The line in the song that says, "Two lovers kissed and the world stood still," is a sweet sentiment, and I do remember mine and

Linda's first kiss. I don't know about the world standing still, but I do know that my heart stopped beating; and again, I did not walk to my car but floated. However, all those endearing moments were totally shattered by our breaking up. A current song at that time that was speaking a lot to me was Jimmy Clanton's April 1958 song, "Just a Dream." "Just a dream, just a dream, all our plans and all our schemes. How could I think you'd be mine, the lies I'd tell myself each time." Yes, those words better described my broken heart. Forget that "many splendored" stuff. Oh, well, life goes on.

After the heart-rending tennis lesson in mid-June, toward the end of the month, Linda called me to invite me to her birthday party that her grandmother was hosting for her in Fort Worth. Sorry, that male pride reared its head again, and I politely said no, thanked her for calling, and hung up. In July, something else occurred to take my mind off my heartache; the other five Cleburne High cheerleaders and I attended the SMU cheerleading school for a week and had a great time. Our group consisted of Tony, Darleene, Sam, Lynda, Sandra, and yours truly. Hey, we came in second place in the mixed group competition!

Then in mid-August, Linda called again and casually suggested our dating once more. The "no" was right on the tip of my tongue, but this time, wonder of wonders, I set my hurt pride aside and said yes. I was on my way to pick her up that Friday evening when disaster struck. I was taking a shortcut from my house on Sabine to East Henderson Street and was coming around this curve, hogging the middle of the street because the shoulder and gutter on the right was under repair. Unfortunately, approaching the curve from the other way was a lady who was also in the middle because her gutter was also torn up. In addition, the empty corner lot on my right (her left) was overgrown with high weeds; neither of us saw the other until it was too late, and we slammed head on without hitting our brakes. Lucky for the both of us, we were only going about fifteen to twenty miles an hour. She had no injuries at all. I had a split lip and a fractured rib, but both front ends of our cars were smashed. I went to the closest house and borrowed their phone. I first called Linda to explain that we would have to postpone the date, then I called my dad (boy,

I dreaded that), and then I called the police. Do you suppose that wreck was an omen regarding our future?

Anyway, we were back together again, and that fall was a blur of dates, football games, and more dates. As the spring rolled around, our romance was thriving. (Oh, sure, we had some arguments now and then, but we always kissed and made up. I kept my stupid pride in check.) As May came and graduation was approaching, a perplexing problem arose. Linda's parents were going to send her to summer school to start college early at Abilene Christian. In addition, there was a further complication. Linda's former boyfriend, the Fort Worth guy, was also going to be in summer school there, finishing up his degree. Linda's grandmother had paid for his four years of college, and of course, he was practically handpicked by her as the right one for Linda. Now as the saying goes, "My momma didn't raise no fool." (Well, remembering my past, y'all could probably dispute that.) Anyway, I could see the handwriting on the wall. With Linda separated from me all summer and close to her ex, Linda's family was evidently hoping that I would be eliminated from the scene permanently. However, I had other plans.

A young couple in Texas could not get married on their own if one of them was under eighteen; he or she would have to have the signed permission of the parents. Linda was only sixteen; she had gone to summer school for three years and thus was able to graduate from high school in three years instead of four. Now her parents would certainly not give their permission, so there was only one thing left for us to do. Scuttlebutt had it that a couple could go to Oklahoma and get married in one day. I told Linda that that was what we would have to do, and she agreed. Thus, we began making our plans. Graduation took place at the end of May, so we set our runaway date during the week prior, on Wednesday, May 20. I asked my sister Melba if I could borrow her car and told her what we were planning to do. My big sister always tried to watch after her little brother, and she knew this was something I really wanted, so she agreed. My parents were not at home at this time; Dad had been severely injured in a car accident in February of that year, 1959. He had been in a coma for three weeks and was not expected to live, but

God answered our prayers, and he came out of it. He was now in the VA hospital in Dallas, and Mom was there with him.

The big day arrived, and I was parked behind the high school, awaiting Linda's arrival. Her mother and she pulled up at the front of the school, and Linda was carrying a large box. She had told her mother the box contained her chorus gown for the Music Club was having pictures taken that day. In reality, the box held her white wedding gown. Up the front steps she walked, through the school, and down the back steps to my sister's car; and off we went—destination, Ardmore, Oklahoma. It was about a two-and-a-half to three-hour drive, and we arrived a little bit before eleven o'clock. We headed straight for the courthouse and the marriage license office. The young man asked us how old we were, and I told him I was twenty-one and Linda was eighteen. He asked to see my driver's license; I reached for my wallet in my back pocket but stopped and told him I had forgotten to bring my wallet. He looked at us, smiled, and said, "Okay, let me have five dollars for the license." I nodded, pulled out my wallet, and handed him a five-dollar bill. He stamped the license, and Linda and I headed for the Church of Christ building that a sign had indicated (she and I were both members at the Central congregation in Cleburne). When we arrived there, the secretary informed us that all the ministers in town were at a preachers' luncheon at a downtown restaurant. We located it and parked outside, waiting for the first man in a suit to come out. One did in a few minutes, and we nabbed him, a Presbyterian, and we followed him to his church building. His wife and his secretary served as our witnesses and took some pictures for us with Linda's camera. We bid them goodbye and headed south to Cleburne.

It was 12:30 p.m., and I had to have Linda back by the time school let out at 3:45 p.m. I floorboarded Melba's 1956, six-cylinder Chevy, and we pulled up at the back of the high school at 3:48 p.m. Linda got out of the car with her gown back in the box, walked through the school, and down the front steps into her mother's car. Brother, was God watching over us!

We graduated the next week, and on the weekend, Linda's parents drove her to Abilene and enrolled her in summer school, where she stayed in a dorm. Meanwhile, my cheerleading buddy Sam had told me that the Texas Lime Plant south of town was hiring, so I applied and got a job loading eighty-pound sacks of calcium on a two-wheel dolly. There were two of us working at the machine, filling the sacks, and then we would wheel the dolly into a boxcar and start filling it up. Naturally, that string of boxcars seemed to stretch from Cleburne to Joshua. However, the job paid well, and that was all I was interested in. Linda had already set us up a bank account in Abilene for I was planning on joining her in the fall when I had saved enough money. One week I would mail her one entire check; the next week I would cash the check and keep out a bare minimum for me to buy my essentials, and then I would mail her the rest in a cashier's check. Plus, I was working as much overtime as I could get, sometimes twelve to fourteen hours a day plus on Saturdays too so I could send her as much money as possible. In June, I was able to see her a couple of times when the boyfriend of her best friend, who was also attending ACC, would travel to Abilene and let me ride with him. Otherwise, I stayed pretty lonely, although we would talk on the phone once or twice a week when Linda would call me from a payphone there in the dorm. Some of the time, she couldn't catch me because I would be working overtime. In addition, we would write each other two or three times a week. To be exact, my letters brought about the climax of our secret marriage.

We really had not thought too much about when and where we would reveal what we had done to her parents. We supposed that that would occur when I joined her in the fall. However, the secret was discovered a little sooner than that. Toward the end of July, I was home from work, getting a bite to eat and cleaning up a bit before I drove back out there to put in some overtime. The phone rang, and I thought, "Oh, boy, I get to talk to Linda for a little bit!" Well, it was Linda all right, but she had some disturbing news.

She said, "Darling, my parents were just here and found out about the wedding. Daddy picked up one of my textbooks before I could stop him, and a letter from you fell out, signed 'Your darling husband.' They had been going to California on a vacation, but now they're returning to Cleburne to see you."

I said, "Goodbye. I'm headed to Mexico!" (Me and my sense of humor.) We shakily said goodbye and hung up. Holy mackerel! What was I going to do? I got on some clean work clothes and prepared to leave when the phone rang again. Uh-oh, this could not be good.

Sure enough, it was Linda's dad. He said they would be back in Cleburne in a couple of hours and were coming by my house to see me. I said, "I'm sorry, but I'm working overtime this evening. I'm heading out to the lime plant right now."

He replied, "That's all right. I know where it is. Please bring that marriage license."

With much trepidation, I drove to the plant and started my shift, dreading what was to come but determined to fight, if necessary, for what I wanted. Sure enough, a couple of hours later, I heard a horn honking outside. I hesitated for a minute, thinking it might be someone else, but another worker stuck his head around the corner and said, "Hey, Weldon, there's somebody in a yellow Plymouth wanting to talk to you." Well, I knew who that Plymouth belonged to, so I took that long walk out to their car, expecting to see that shotgun protruding from the window as I got closer. However, Linda's dad was quite cordial, considering the circumstances, and merely asked to see the marriage license. I politely reached in my shirt pocket and handed it to him. He read over it and then asked me, "You two have sure aged fast, haven't you?"

A flippant retort was right on the tip of my tongue like, "Marriage will do that to you," but believe it or not, this time, I kept my big mouth shut and said nothing.

Then he commented, "You realize that I could have this annulled?"

I replied, "Yes, sir, I do, but we would simply do it again."

He wryly smiled and said, "That's what I thought. Let us think about this. Linda is coming home this weekend, and we'll all sit down together and talk this over."

I said okay, after asking for the marriage license back, and they drove off.

That Saturday, I drove out to Linda's, and the four of us had a rather awkward conversation about her and me, and what the future held for us. Her parents reluctantly agreed to our marriage, and I suppose you could say her father and I called a tenuous truce which lasted for twenty-six years, but that's another story.

# CHAPTER 31

# HOW TO BECOME AN ENGLISH TEACHER

In high school or college, did you have those teachers who thought they were born to be English teachers, even God ordained, if you will? So did I. Boy, they took their calling so seriously and expected us to do the same. Now it just so happens that I am an English teacher and have taught that subject for fifty-three years. Yikes, that's a long time. However, when I graduated from Cleburne High in May of 1959, trust me, English was not going to be my major in college.

When I enrolled in Abilene Christian College in September of 1959, chemistry was my major. I had taken that class my senior year and thoroughly enjoyed it, making an *A* in it. Thus, I thought it would be a fascinating and enjoyable career, becoming a chemist, chemical engineer, or pharmacist. Oh, well. "The best laid plans of mice and men," as they say. The lecture portion of the college class was okay; I could always memorize when I applied myself. However, the chemistry lab was another story. Picture Jerry Lewis in *The Nutty Professor*. Whatever could go wrong did go wrong. For example, I would heat a test tube and, with a set of tongs, set the tube in the rack to cool. Someone would say something to me, and after answering them, I would turn back to the rack, forgetting that the tube was still too hot. Bumbling me would pick it up, burning my fingers and dropping the test tube on the floor, thus ruining whatever experiment I had been running. Another favorite habit of mine was to drop concentrated sulfuric acid on one of my hands and watch it just about sear its way down to the bone. In addition, my lab instructor was an absolute fiend. He would always give us these "unknowns" in a test tube, and we had to run different tests on them to try to discover what the unknown was. Naturally, I was rarely successful. At the end of the semester, the instructor confessed to me that half the time, he had given me water as the unknown, just to watch me hurriedly run a half a dozen tests, unsuccessfully, I might add. Needless to say, my ardor toward this career major was waning.

After one year at Abilene Christian, my wife and I moved back to Cleburne, where I began working full time at Fort Worth Steel and Machinery on McCart Street in Fort Worth while attending the University of Texas at Arlington part time. By now, I had changed my major to nice, bland business; so I'm taking economics, business math, and accounting. The latter I wound up dropping for the simple reason that it was primarily a math class, and I don't like math. With not being too pleased with my new major, I was therefore intrigued, when passing the counseling offices at UTA, to see a sign saying, "Free Aptitude Tests." Hey, I'll do anything free, right? Into the door I went and took a couple of hours of tests and left.

I came back the next week so the counselor could explain the results to me. He told me that I scored high in English and history and asked me why I did not major in one of those. "What would I do if I majored in English?" I inquired.

He replied, "You could become an English teacher."

"What?" I exclaimed. "The most detested profession on the face of the earth except for the Internal Revenue?"

"Well," the counselor stated, "if you still like the sciences (which I did and still do), you could major in English with a special emphasis on technical writing. Then you could work for some chemical company, writing articles or operating manuals, stuff like that." That certainly sounded appealing, more so than a dreaded career of nearly everyone's archenemy, an English teacher.

For the third time, I changed my major, this time to English but geared toward technical writing. Now there was a slight problem here which the counselor had failed to point out. There were only two technical writing courses offered, Tech I and Tech II. Yet to major in a particular area, you had to complete a minimum of thirty hours in that subject. With technical writing only offering six hours, I had to fill up the other twenty-four hours in straight English courses, freshman composition and the rest in literature, which I dutifully did, finishing with thirty-six hours total in English.

In my junior year, I transferred to North Texas State University in Denton, since we had moved to Wise County. In the last semester of my senior year, I was just taking various courses to complete my Bachelor's degree requirement of 120 hours. With six weeks left in the semester, I was taking job interviews with a technical writing emphasis. I turned down one offer from Dow Chemical because they wanted me to move to Boston, of all places. What? Me, a native Texan, move to Beantown, six months of winter? Not on your life. I had one final interview scheduled with a gentleman from the Health, Education, and Welfare Department. I had dropped off my resume the previous week and came back to see what his offer was. He said, "Reed, you're just the man for the job—English major, *A* in speech. The job is yours if you want it."

"What is this job, specifically?" I asked.

He explained to me that a national epidemic was about to break out, and the government wanted to nip it in the bud. They had composed a slide show with an accompanying script. All I had to do was memorize the script, delivering it with the slide show as I toured the country. In doing so, I would actually be saving lives.

"Okay." I asked, "What is this national epidemic?"

Without changing his composure, he calmly replied, "Venereal disease."

"What!" I exclaimed. "You want me to become a national authority on VD?"

He said, "Yes."

I said, "No!" and walked out.

The next day, I related this humorous encounter with the HEW representative to one of my favorite English teachers at NTSU, who laughed uproariously. Then he asked, "Weldon, are you still looking for a job?"

"Yes," I replied.

He stated, "We have one Master's fellowship left. Why don't you apply for it? I'll recommend you."

Hey, I'm just an ol' country boy from Cleburne. I had to ask him, "What is a Master's fellowship?"

He replied, "It's a graduate grant. We pay your tuition and buy your books for you. Plus you will be teaching two Composition I classes for us, and we'll pay you one thousand dollars per class."

"What do I do with a Master's degree in English?" I inquired.

He answered, "You can teach English in college."

I pondered my choices—a national authority on VD or a college English teacher? You know my decision. I graduated with my Bachelor's degree in May of 1963, and in September of that same year, I stood in front of my first English class. You talk about students being nervous on the first day!

I completed my Master's degree in a year and a half. When I was completing my thesis, this same NTSU teacher informed me that TCU was offering a doctoral fellowship, a three-year grant, and I should apply for it. He would give me another recommendation. This time, I did not have to ask what a fellowship was. Thus,

I applied, and sure enough, landed the fellowship. I worked on my doctorate there at TCU for three years, taking eighteen classes; but darn it, I was not successful in passing the comprehensive exams, five days of testing over any and all aspects of world literature.

Oh, well, for this old country boy from Cleburne, acquiring a Master's degree and three years' work toward my doctorate wasn't too bad. Who would have thought that I would become an English teacher, but now, I *are* one!

# CHAPTER 32

# BEBE DOG THE HUNTER

Do dogs go to heaven? Oh, I certainly hope so! I think back about the various pet dogs that I have had and would so love to see them again: Blackie, my shepherd mix when I was a kid growing up in Cleburne; Grendal, my beautiful German shepherd when I lived in Paradise, Texas, in Wise County; Buck, my magnificent Alaskan malamute who just walked into my garage when I was living in North Richland Hills; and Gussie, my wonderful black Lab when I lived in Weatherford. Of course, the two worthless varmints that I now own, Button and Baby Girl, are another story. They are what my wife and I call rat huahuas, half rat terrier and half Chihuahua. They are brother and sister, and we have had them five years now. We might as well have gone ahead and adopted two children; they are that much trouble. However, I want to describe a precious dog that I acquired my first year in college in 1959—Bebe the Hunter.

Bebe was a rat terrier, and we paid thirty-five dollars for him from a family in Haslet. That was the first time in my life that I gave actual money for a dog. In the past, you just picked up a stray somewhere, but Linda's parents had bought a terrier from these people, so we did too. Several years later, we moved to Wise County to live on a small ranch that Linda's grandmother had given her dad (about four hundred acres or so) where he began to raise Angus cattle. Meanwhile, Linda and I were commuting to North Texas State University for her to complete her education degree and me to finish my English degree.

Now this acreage was absolutely infested with armadillos. We would be driving across any pasture in the pickup, and suddenly, one of the front wheels would drop down into an armadillo den. Pop suggested that we begin an eradication program, so several evenings a week, when I arrived home from college, I would grab my .22 rifle, and off I would go with my dog Bebe and Herman, a border collie belonging to my father-in-law (Herman has a unique story himself, but I'll save that one for another time). We would always jump up several armadillos and a jackrabbit or two every now and then. I could always hit the lumbering armadillos, but the jackrabbits were another story. Up the jackrabbit would jump, the dogs would give chase, I would fire and miss, the jackrabbit would run out of sight with Bebe in hot pursuit. Herman would usually give up pretty quickly, and Bebe might; but more times than not, he would be gone for an hour or more and come home totally exhausted. That was the typical hunting routine for quite a while until I got smart and bought a single barrel, 16-gauge shotgun. The first time I carried it, sure enough, a jackrabbit burst out ahead of us. The dogs gave chase, I fired, and the rabbit tumbled over, dead. Meanwhile, the dogs ran right on by it; they were so accustomed to my missing it. I had to call them back, and I suppose they were rightly impressed.

On some occasions, Bebe was not quite as ferocious as he tried to act. One night, I remember hearing a scratching noise on our wooden front porch. The porch light was on, so I peered out the window in the door, and there was an armadillo wandering around on the porch. Well, I knew how to run that critter off, so I called Bebe over to the door, opened it and the screen door, and said, "Sic 'em, Bebe," expecting a full-scale battle to ensue right there in front of me. However, a slight problem arose; Bebe rushed out on the porch all right, but the armadillo just ignored him and continued to wander around. Bebe looked at me with this strange look on his face, "Hey, isn't he supposed to run away in dreaded fear of me?" When the armadillo did not take off in fright, Bebe found this boring and just turned around and came back in the house.

Another wildlife encounter did not quite go as Bebe had planned either. My wife, kids, mother-in-law, and I were vacationing down in Port Aransas while my father-in-law remained at home. Bebe would stay up at the big house with Pop and Herman anytime we were gone for any length of time. Pop did not like cats and especially domestic cats that were running wild, considering them as a threat to baby quail. Thus, he would trap them in those large, cage-like traps and get rid of them. On this occasion, he checked the trap by his garage, and sure enough, there was a snarling, unhappy cat in it. Pop thought he would have some fun, so he called the two dogs over and opened the trap door. The enraged cat immediately took off down the gravel driveway with both dogs in hot pursuit. Now Bebe was a little faster than Herman, whose right rear leg was a little withered from a prior accident. Thus, Bebe was hot after the cat with his nose close to the cat's tail as the cat approached the nearest tree. Bless Bebe's heart; I'm sure he thought the cat was going to scamper up into the tree, but no. Instead, the cat turned around with his back to the tree and prepared for battle. On seeing this, Bebe attempted to stop but could not do so on the loose gravel, and he slid right into the awaiting feline, who was just about as big as Bebe. With paws and fangs flashing, the cat had Bebe bleeding from his muzzle and ears in no time flat and would probably have done much worse except our hero Herman jumped into the fray, grabbing the cat by the back, breaking its spine.

One last hunting experience comes to mind, one that displayed Bebe's grit and determination. The two dogs and I were trekking through this dry creek bed when they disappeared around a bend in the creek. Suddenly, I heard this ferocious barking break out, indicating the dogs had discovered something. I quickly trotted around the corner, and the dogs were digging and barking at this small hole in the side of the creek bed. I shooed the dogs aside and started enlarging the hole with my hands so Bebe might be able to crawl inside and see if he could drag out whatever was in there. When the hole was big enough, I held Bebe by the shoulders and started getting him excited about charging down that hole. "Sic 'em, Bebe. Get him, boy. Tear him up." All four of Bebe's legs were digging into the ground, eager to launch himself down the hole, so I turned him loose; and he shot down that hole, out of sight. I could hear him growling and snarling at something. I thought it was probably another armadillo or maybe a stray cat.

Then I saw Bebe's hindquarters appear, jerking as if he were dragging something. I stepped back to give him room and to give me the space needed to shoot whatever he was bringing out of there. Sure enough, here came Bebe's shoulders, then his head and mouth. He had in his mouth a black-and-white tail; he was pulling a *skunk* out of that hole! Naturally, I ran backward for about ten yards to not get sprayed by Pepe Le Pew, but Bebe was not that fortunate. The skunk had got him good, and my poor dog was slobbering and frothing at the mouth while rolling over and over on the ground. Meanwhile, the skunk had at first darted back in the hole, but then he made the fatal mistake to stick his head back out to see what was going on. I promptly shot him in the throat, and he jerked back into the hole, out of sight.

By now, Bebe had staggered to his feet, and looking at him, I got an idea. The skunk was surely dead back in the hole, and Bebe could not be sprayed again by a dead skunk. Thus, I started getting him excited again by saying, "Sic 'em, Bebe Dog. Get him, boy," and sure enough, back into the hole he went. About a minute later, he backed out of the hole with his dead quarry. Instantly, he and Herman attacked the dead skunk like it was the most vicious creature on earth.

Yes, that was my wonderful, faithful hunting buddy and lap dog, who shared my life for thirteen years. Then, sadly, as often happens, he was run over by a car in front of my house when I was living in Paradise, Texas, in Wise County, where I preached part time for the Church of Christ congregation there. We have all lost our four-legged family members, and it absolutely shreds our hearts, doesn't it? There is a poem by Robinson Jeffers that I would recommend you look up online entitled, "The House Dog's Grave." Jeffers had lost his canine companion and wrote this poem from the viewpoint of the dead dog, speaking to him from his little grave just outside the poet's study window. The last stanza states:

> You were never masters, but friends. I was your
> friend.
> I loved you well, and was loved. Deep love
> endures
> To the end and far past the end. If this is
> my end,
> I am not lonely. I am not afraid. I am still
> yours. (1941)

# CHAPTER 33

# HERMAN THE WONDER DOG

Have you ever seen a dog walking on just its front paws with its hind legs hoisted up in the air? That was my introduction to Herman, a border collie that I referred to in my previous story about my rat terrier, Bebe. In that story, Herman saved Bebe's life by dispatching this large cat that was ripping Bebe to shreds. Herman's own story begins in 1961 when my father-in-law and I were driving back to his house after picking up some items at the feed store in Cleburne. We were on Highway 4 about a mile past Rose Hill Cemetery when we saw this unusual sight in the ditch alongside the highway. This dog was actually walking along on just its front paws. Evidently, it had been struck by a car, but it courageously was managing to survive, I suppose, by scavenging on what scraps or carrion it could find in the ditch.

Pop pulled his pickup over just past the dog, and when we stopped, the dog lowered itself to the ground, waiting to see, I guess, what we were up to. Pop said the dog had to be in severe pain and that I should go knock it in the head with a hammer from his tool-box. I replied, "Not on your life!" He did not want to do it either, so we sat there pondering for a few minutes.

Then he stated, "Weldon, go see if he will let you pick him up and set him in the bed of the pickup." Notice he volunteered *me* for the task. I wasn't too keen on the idea, figuring I was about to get my hand or face bitten off; but if it was going to help the dog, I was willing. Pop stated that if I could do that, we would turn around, take him to the vet on the corner of South Main and Country Club Road, and have the poor animal humanely put to sleep. I quite cautiously approached the dog and knelt just in front of him. He gave no indication of viciousness, so I slowly reached out my hand to him so he could sniff the back of it, which he did, and then he licked it. Now I knew I had made a friend. I very carefully slipped my arms underneath his front shoulders and lifted him up, putting as little pressure as possible on his hindquarters. Pop had an old tarp in the back of the pickup, which he had folded over for a bed for the dog, and I gently laid him on it. He whimpered a little, but that was all. We did a U-turn and slowly drove back into Cleburne to the vet's office. I repeated the process of picking the dog up and took him inside to the examination room. The doctor confirmed for us that both its back legs were broken. Pop instructed him to have the dog put to sleep and send him the bill, and then we left and began the trip home.

We had not even reached the cemetery when Pop pulled over and stopped. He looked at me and stated, "That dog is really too brave and courageous to just be put to sleep. He deserves a fighting chance at life, whatever quality of life that might be for him." Having said that, he did another U-turn, and back to the vet's office we flew. Fortunately, the doctor had not performed the procedure yet, and Pop instructed him to do whatever he could to save the dog's life, regardless of the cost. We then drove home. Later, the vet called the house and said he had put two aluminum casts on the dog's hind legs, and time would tell if the legs would heal or not. He stated that the dog had a strong constitution and was sure a fighter, so he would certainly survive physically. The condition of his legs would be another story.

In a week, the doctor called to tell us we could come and pick him up, which we did. Thus began about a ten-year relationship with this unusual dog that Pop had named Herman. We had fixed him a bed of old blankets in one corner of the garage. We didn't think he would run away, not in his condition; but would you believe he still continued to walk on his front legs while hoisting his hind legs, aluminum casts and all, up in the air? After several weeks, the doctor instructed us to remove the casts and see what the dog could do. His left hind leg had healed completely, although his right leg was a little shorter than the other, though healthy. Again, for a time, even with the casts off, Herman would still walk on his front legs only, but then he gradually began walking on all four legs and even running. He was not as fast as Bebe was, but he could stay close to my terrier, and they became best buddies.

In 1962, we moved to Pop's ranch in Wise County, between Bridgeport and Cottondale, where the two dogs and I began to combat the armadillo infestation problem. For some reason, it seemed that Herman absolutely hated armadillos. I could be in our house studying for my classes at North Texas State University, and I would hear Herman barking in the distance. I would grab my .22 rifle, and Bebe and I would tear out of the house to see what Herman was up to. Invariably, he would have an armadillo down a hole and would be doing his best to dig it out. Most of the time, Herman would be successful in doing so. If not, hopefully, I would hear him if I were home and come running to help him out. If I weren't home and he could not dig the critter out, he would gnaw off the armadillo's tail as far down as he could reach. I was always coming across stub-tailed armadillos all over the ranch.

One particular incident comes to mind. The whole family was crappie fishing at this tank on the back side of the ranch. Everybody was pulling in fish but me. I could set my bobber with its minnow right beside my wife's, and hers would go down while mine just sat there. Boring! Suddenly, I heard Herman barking nearby; and eager for any excuse to give up this frustrating exercise in futility, I dropped my pole and took off jogging to find him. Sure enough, about a hundred yards away, he was digging away at this hole and barking furiously. I shooed him away and looked down in the hole. There was the back and tail of the largest armadillo that I had ever seen. The diameter of his tail was about as wide as my wrist. I was going to have a tussle on my hands if I were going to be successful in pulling him out of that hole using solely brute strength (I'm not that big of a brute). So I sat down on my derriere, propped my feet on both sides of the hole, grabbed his tail in both hands, and the tug of war commenced. Now the armadillo has the advantage in this struggle. First of all, he is digging in with all four paws; I only have two. In addition, in that situation, I have been told that the varmint raises its scales so that they dig into the ceiling and sides of the hole. My only chance to pull him out by muscle alone is if I can manage to also grab one of his hind legs. If I can do that, he is mine.

So I'm sitting there on the ground, involved in this herculean tug of war, straining with all I've got, when I hear Herman barking again. I look around, and believe it or not, he is running another armadillo straight for this particular hole! Unbelievably, this second armadillo runs under my legs and is scratching away at the first armadillo, trying to get in the same hole. What do I do? I grabbed the second armadillo with one hand while still holding on to the bigger one with the other hand and slammed the second one on the ground, stunning it. Herman then pounced on it while I returned to my battle with the larger armadillo. Sure enough, I was able to grab a hind leg and got him out of there, where I turned him over to Herman too.

That remarkable dog lived another eight or nine years, joyously chasing armadillos all over the ranch. He died peacefully in his sleep and is probably still chasing armadillos in dog heaven. I hope to see him again one day.

# CHAPTER 34

# THE PERILS OF PARENTING

Regardless of what modern-day psychologists tell us, God made boys different from girls. With my two daughters, all I had to do was say something sternly to them and that would put them in tears. However, with my three sons, trying to get a point across to them was like talking to the wall. I did have some memorable moments with Tim, my oldest son, and Jim, my middle son.

With Tim, I seemed to have a problem keeping track of the boy, where he was at the moment. One occasion resulted in my wife and me having to visit the police station in Haltom City. When Tim was about four or five, we were hosting a church party for young married couples at our house on Nadine Street. There were ten or twelve couples there with about that many kids, some Tim's age, with some a little older or younger. It was at night, and the parents were in the house, visiting, while some of the youngsters were playing inside and others outside in the backyard illuminated by the patio lights. By ten o'clock, everybody was leaving, and we parents gathered up all the children. Uh-oh. Tim was missing! My wife and I frantically searched through the house and then the backyard—still no sign of our four-year-old.

We had two gates in our backyard. The west one totally lit up by our patio lights and locked, and the east one on the far side of the house, unlocked but totally in darkness. I never dreamed any of the kids would wander over there. When I investigated this gate, it was ajar. Oh, no. Tim had wandered off somewhere! I immediately took off running down the hill west toward Stanley-Keller Road while my wife got in the car and drove the other way, east up Nadine. I hit Stanley-Keller and turned right, looking frantically everywhere and yelling Tim's name. Suddenly, a Haltom police car pulled up beside me, and the officer inside asked me what the problem was. I told him, and he said, "Sir, we have your son down at the police station. One of our officers picked him up, wandering down Stanley-Keller about a block from here. Would you and your wife follow me down to the station?" Naturally, I agreed to his request, and he drove me back up Nadine where we found Linda, and off we went. She and I were so relieved and thanked God that Tim was all right. Of course, he was crying his heart out when we arrived, but his mother and I quickly smothered him with hugs and kisses, taking care of that problem. However, another problem arose. The police read us the riot act about not properly watching our child, which of course, I could understand. We left there, hopefully, as wiser parents. One act of wisdom involved putting locks on both of our backyard gates anytime we had a party.

Would you believe that I lost Tim again about two years later? This time, it was solely my fault. My wife and I, along with Cindy, our oldest child at the time, and Tim went to downtown Fort Worth to do some shopping at Stripling's Department Store. Linda and Cindy were strolling through the women's section while I had Tim with me as I ambled through the men's area, looking at shoes, shirts, and suits. Tim kept running in and out of the racks of clothing, and I finally had had enough. I took him by the hand and led him to a chair right beside the fitting area. I told him, "Stay there until I come and get you! Do you understand me?" He glumly nodded his head, and I walked back over to the suits to see what they might have on sale. I spent ten minutes or so there; then I saw Linda and Cindy a couple of aisles over, so I caught up to them and strolled beside them for a few minutes. Linda then turned to me, looked all around me, and asked quizzically, "Where is Tim?" I turned around, momentarily puzzled; then it dawned on me where I had left him. I frantically ran back to the men's suits area, and sure enough, there he sat on that chair where I had left him, though with tears running down his face, probably thinking that his dad had deserted him. Of course, I knelt and hugged him, apologizing for leaving him alone so long. I also praised him for being so obedient to stay exactly where I had left him.

Now my son Jim was not quite as well behaved as Tim usually was. Even at the tender age of one and a half, Jim posed a challenge for me, not in obedience but in clean-up duty. At the time, I was teaching at Tarrant County College—South Campus. I taught on Monday-Wednesday-Friday days and Tuesday-Thursday nights. Thus, I stayed home with Jim on Tuesday-Thursday days. After lunch, Jim was in his baby crib in his room napping while I was in my study, grading papers. What else does a poor English teacher do at home? I spend about seventy percent of my time at home grading. After about an hour of peace and quiet coming from Jim's room, I now heard giggling and laughing. "Hmm, is this good or bad? He is at least occupied," I said to myself. However, I thought I had better investigate. I nonchalantly walked into his room and just about fainted! He had filled up his diaper with some solid material and used it to *paint* everything—yes, the entire crib but also the entire length of the wall that he could reach! Help! What did I do? Well, first I pushed his crib outside onto the patio (fortunately, this was in the fall, and the temperature was warm). I then brought the water hose over and commenced to wash the crib and Jim at the same time. Naturally, he enjoyed that and thought it was great fun! Afterward, I dried off the crib (and Jim) with towels, trundled him back inside the house, and parked him just outside his room where I faced another clean-up chore. I finally got the wall clean and the carpet with Jim encouraging me all the time with his giggling and more laughter. Could he have possibly done this all on purpose just to torment me?

One final episode involving Jim taught me a lesson in proper parenting that I will never forget, and it still hurts me today when I remember the judgmental blunder that I made. Jim was eleven years old and in the fifth grade. Report cards had come in the day before, and it was our custom for the kids to show them to Linda and me the next morning at the breakfast table. Laura showed us hers, all *A*'s, as usual. Then I asked Jim where his was. He answered, "Dad, I couldn't find it this morning."

I stated, "Son, that is so lame. Get in your room and find that thing before you leave for school in thirty minutes or I'm going to give you five licks with my black belt. (Yes, I believed in corporal punishment and still do!)

Sure enough, the time for him to leave for school came and no report card. I went to my closet, retrieved my belt, and had him follow me to my study where I administered the five licks, and he went to school.

That afternoon, I arrived home before he did, and I had been bothered by the report card thing all day. The boy had seemed so honest in his denial; thus, I started searching his room carefully to see if he had actually misplaced the card. I even dared to move out his bed and look under there amidst all the accumulated trash of weeks, if not months, but still no card. I then walked out of his room, happened to glance to the right into Laura's room, and noticed a pile of clean clothes in the corner that she was supposed to have folded before she left for school. "Oh, good grief," I thought. I walked over, picked up the entire pile, and set it all on her bed to remind her of the chore when she arrived home. As I turned back toward the door, I happened to notice something white lying on the floor in the corner where the clean clothes had been. I stepped over and picked up Jim's report card (yes, with all *A*'s, as always). Ouch!

I then went to my closet, grabbed my black belt, and then brought it with me to my study and laid it on one corner of my desk. I began grading once more (as always) for about an hour when I heard Jim enter the back door and come into the living room, whistling as he did so. I called out to him to come to my study, and he walked in. "Yeah, Dad?" he inquired.

I told him, "Son, here is your report card. You had lost it just as you said. It was underneath a pile of clothes in Laura's room. I'm sorry. I wrongfully gave you five licks, thinking you were lying to me. Take my belt there and give me ten licks just as hard as you can to teach me a lesson." I then leaned forward over the desk, awaiting my proper punishment.

Jim looked at me for a few seconds before stating, "Aww, Dad, I can't do that!" Brother, his refusal hurt me worse than the spanking would have done. Instead, I hugged him and told him I would try to have more faith in him in the future.

We endeavor to teach our children right from wrong, but sometimes they do a pretty good job of teaching us too, don't they?

# CHAPTER 35

# FOND MEMORIES OF LIFE ON SABINE STREET

"Memries light the corners of my mind," as Barbra Streisand sang it. Yes, I know "memries" is misspelled there, but that is how she pronounced it in singing it, so I will remain faithful to her. We all have memories of our childhoods, some good and some bad, but they all played a role in making us who we are today. I have some affectionate ones that I experienced growing up on the northeast side of town.

One favorite memory I have involved the old ice trucks. Now I doubt if too many folks on the west side would remember those since those citizens probably owned real, electric-powered refrigerators in the late 1940s and early 1950s.

My family did not; we owned a true "ice box." It was a wooden container about four feet high and two feet wide, tin lined inside, with a small door on top and a larger door on the front. You pulled on the handle on the small top door to reveal a metal compartment that held the block of ice that cooled the rest of the box. When you pulled on the handle on the larger front door, it would open and reveal three to four smaller compartments that held the various foodstuffs.

The Cleburne Ice House was on Border Street, I believe, near downtown; and the ice trucks would load up there and scatter out over town, distributing their loads to various neighborhoods just like the newspaper folks would. I remember we would place a square cardboard sign in one of our front windows. This sign had four numbers listed, one on each of the four sides. I believe ours had the numbers 5, 10, 25, and 50, each number representing the pounds of ice that we wanted that day. We usually wanted 25 pounds, so we would place our sign with the number 25 at the top, and the iceman would know to bring that size from his truck.

When the truck would stop in front of our house, the fun would commence. The iceman would get out of his truck, walk to the back of it, and lift the rubber flap that covered the back to grab his ice hook and latch on to the block of ice that Mom had ordered. Then he would hoist the block up on his shoulder and carry it into the house to place it in our icebox. As soon as he disappeared, one of us kids (ten to twelve years old at the time) would hop up into the back of the truck and start handing out pieces of ice that had broken off from the blocks. When the iceman came out the front door, naturally, we would take off running. I remember a time or two when he came out and I was still in the truck, so I would duck down behind one of the larger blocks while he would throw his ice hook in the back, drop the rubber flap, and get in his truck and start to drive off. I would then slip out of the back and join my buddies. The summer before my brother Eldon's senior year, he worked at the ice house—a "cool" job, I must say, but pretty rigorous horsing those seventy-five to one-hundred-pound blocks of ice onto conveyor belts and then into the ice trucks.

Speaking of "horsing around," another memory or two of mine did involve horses, one episode a little scary, and the other rather exciting. The scary moment occurred one summer morning (I was about ten or twelve) when some buddies and I were visiting one of our neighbors down the street who owned four or five horses that he would sometimes let us ride inside his horse pen if we didn't mind doing so bareback. That didn't bother me and my buddy Ronnie, so he and I were jogging around the lot on two of the horses, having a fun time. I was riding this large white mare who had this young colt trotting alongside her. I was paying no attention to what the colt was doing when it suddenly reached up and bit me in my right ribcage. I guess he was jealous or hungry. I immediately jerked back on the reins, which caused the mare to rear up. Then she lost her balance and fell over backward! Fortunately, I was able to shove away from her to my right, and she missed crushing me flat! Needless to say, that brought a halt to our horseplay.

Until another episode, that is. On another occasion, Ronnie and I were walking down Chase Avenue, one street east of Sabine, heading to our friend Carol's house, when we heard the clip-clopping of horse hooves behind us. We turned around, and here came two horses trotting toward us, both with bridles but no saddles or riders! Hey, like they say, "Bird nest on the ground"! This means, "Look what fortune had dropped into our laps." We immediately walked out in front of the horses and spread our arms out to slow them down. We then hemmed them up in a corner where two fences formed an L; next, we each picked out a horse and hopped up on its back, and away we went for fun and frolic. The next couple of hours, we played as much cowboys and Indians as we wanted to. We had the time of our lives—until we heard some shouting and cursing behind us. Turning around, we saw a rather irate gentleman galloping toward us on another horse, yelling something about, "Stop, you horse thieves!"

I told Ronnie, "He can't chase us and the horses at the same time," so we slid off their backs, slapped them on the rump to head them in one direction, and we took off running in another toward a nearby patch of woods. Luckily, the angry horse owner did take off after his horses. I don't see what he was so mad about. We *rescued* those horses; we didn't steal them.

Lastly, I dearly loved some of those old radio shows that played in the late 1940s through the mid-1950s. Since my family did not have a TV until about the mid-'50s, I listened to a lot of radio at night (after I finished my homework—Mom and Dad would make sure of that). Later, most of those shows were turned into TV shows, but I cherished them on the radio. I remember The Lone Ranger, The Life of Riley, The Great Gildersleeve and his nephew Leroy ("It is I, Digby O'Dell, the friendly undertaker"); Jack Benny and Rochester, Our Miss Brooks, Amos and Andy, Abbot and Costello, The Shadow, Red Skelton and Junior, Fibber McGee and Molly, Dragnet, Boston Blackie ("Friend of those who have no friend, enemy of those who make him an enemy"); and Lum and Abner ("Jot 'Em Down Store, Lum Eddards speaking"). I can still hear some of those voices today. However, I had one favorite that really stood out to me: Sergeant Preston of the Yukon and his trusty sled dog, King. I can hear today, "On, King, on, you huskies." Then he and his faithful dog would track down the latest nefarious scoundrels who were up to no good. At the end of each program, Sergeant Preston would say, "Well, King, this case is closed."

However, this radio show planted an idea in my mind that did not turn out too successful. Some of the sergeant's friends and some of the villains that he chased were trappers. These were men who made money by trapping animals like mink, otter, ermine, minx, and beaver, and selling their hides. Now it just so happened that Daddy had a small varmint trap hanging on the wall out in our storage shed. The idea occurred to me that I could take that trap, walk a ways out into the woods east of town from me, no more than a mile away, and I bet I could find plenty of animals to trap and become rich! I would become the wealthiest ten-year-old in town! I would ride the most expensive bike! I would date all the prettiest girls! Life would be grand! (Sounds a little like my get-rich-quick scheme I had about the cotton patch when I was six, doesn't it?)

Well, the next day after hatching this great plan, I grabbed the varmint trap and took off for the wilds of the country east of town. As I entered the woods, I began searching the ground for animal tracks like the men on Sergeant Preston had done, and sure enough, I spotted some tracks leading in and out of a hole in the ground. All right! First victim and first dollar coming up! I found a stout branch that I broke off to form a stake and with a rock, pounded it into the metal ring on one end of the chain to prevent the animal from dragging off Daddy's trap (he would tan me good if that happened). Then I carefully pried the jaws apart and set the trap. I then went home, eager to return the next morning to start compiling my riches. Sure enough, the next morning, I came to the hole where I had set the trap, and there, caught in trap, was a tremendous prize—a terrapin, a land turtle!

Oh, good grief! It didn't even have any fur on it! How could I sell that thing? Feeling rather guilty for inflicting any pain on that pathetic little creature, I released it and began looking for a more likely hole than that one. After traipsing around the woods for about another half hour, I found another hole and gave it another try—staking the trap down, prying the jaws open, setting the pin, and then trudging home. The next morning, I eagerly made my way to my trap, totally confident that some furry critter would be awaiting me, quite willing to sacrifice its hide to fill my coffers with money. Again, the trap had been sprung; again, the victim was a poor terrapin or box turtle. Again, my get-rich-quick scheme had fizzled. I quit.

# CHAPTER 36

# THE CARNIVORE AND
# THE VEGETARIAN

Where did I go wrong as a parent with my middle son Jim? For the first twenty-one years of his life, he was a normal carnivore, eating any kind of meat placed before him. Well, okay, maybe not liver and onions, which I loved and still do, but he usually cleaned his plate. At twenty-one, however, he changed; and looking back now, I can see that it was my fault.

The root cause for the change began, ironically enough, with my love for football which started in the sixth grade when I played, sparingly, for Irving Elementary. For some reason, that year, I began to associate football with Texas football, that is, the University of Texas football. I would read about them in the paper, listen some on the radio, and generally became a faithful follower. This love affair grew until by the time I reached college, I lived, breathed, and bled burnt orange. I can remember Saturdays in the fall, if I were deer hunting in the early afternoon, I would be sitting in a tree stand or box stand with a transistor radio plugged in my ear, waiting for Bambi to step out and for the Longhorns to win. So yes, UT football was important to me.

Naturally, being an ardent, rabid UT fan, I detested certain other teams who were avowed opponents of theirs. The head of the list, of course, were the despicable Aggies, followed by the loathsome Sooners, and the odious Razorbacks. (Did you hear about the Aggie who moved from Texas to Oklahoma? He raised the IQ level in both states!) My son Jim, of course, was quite aware of my football passions. His first two years of college, he attended Southwest Texas State at San Marcos, majoring in physics (boy, he did not inherit those genes from me). In the summer following his sophomore year, he called me to get my advice. He stated that he wanted to continue and finish his physics degree at San Marcos, but he was considering enrolling also at either A&M or UT to get a double degree in electrical engineering. Since he knew my distaste for the Aggies, he wanted to run his decision by me since he was leaning toward A&M. I answered him quite honestly, "Son, I will admit that A&M's engineering school has a slightly higher reputation than UT's."

"So," he responded, "you won't mind if I enroll at A&M?"

"No," I replied. "I'll just cut you out of my will."

So what happened? He enrolled at UT, which should have thrilled me to death. However, what followed stunned me. After attending UT for a short time, Jim gave up hunting, joined Ralph Nader's Green Party, and became a vegetarian! What had I done to my son? As if all of that were not catastrophic enough, he made attempts to convert *me* to vegetarianism. First, he tried through emailing me. I was sitting at my desk, grading papers, which is about seventy percent of my job as an English teacher, when my wife informed me that Jim had emailed me and I should come read it (we only had one computer at the time for I was trying to avoid becoming enslaved to it). I reluctantly got to my feet and sat down at the computer to read his email, which was about five pages long. It told of the sad story of this heavily overweight cattle rancher in Colorado who pumped steroids into his cows to make them weigh more and bring more money at the market. Then "Hallelujah!" He and his cows were saved. He sold off all the cattle and let his ranch revert to nature. Plus, he himself became a vegetarian and lost one hundred pounds!

Naturally, I saw through my son's scheme and responded with the following retort. "Nice try, son. Fat chance. I plan on being buried with a 32-ounce T-bone between my teeth!"

However, he was persistent. The next time he visited me, he started a physiological study with me about man's colon and how it was not designed to properly digest meat. Instead, the meat would collect in the coils of the colon and deteriorate, causing cancer.

I stopped him there and said, "Son, let me ask you a couple of physiological questions of my own. What is the largest, flabbiest, fattest, if you will, land mammal on earth? Answer, yes, the elephant! And what does an elephant eat? That's right. He's a vegetarian! Now, second question. What is the sleekest, skinniest, fastest land animal on earth? That's right, the cheetah! And what is the diet of the cheetah? Aha? A carnivore! Now pray tell me where are the elephant's eyes located, as are cows, pigs, chickens, Bambi, etc.? On the sides of their heads. Why? Because they are prey animals and have to watch out for those carnivores who want to eat them! Now, son, the clincher. Where are the eyes of the cheetah located, as are the eyes of lions, tigers, cougars, cats, dogs, *man*! That's right. At the front, looking for those animals we are supposed to eat, just like God made us! Case closed!"

# CHAPTER 37

## AEROPHOBIA AND ME

I read that twenty-five percent of humans have a fear of flying. I know, I know—we also are twenty-nine times safer flying than driving a car. However, that still doesn't comfort me a whole lot. Of course, my fear used to be worse, and now it has evolved into more of an apprehension about flying. But consider how my challenge is compounded by the fact that I have a combination of phobias: mild claustrophobia, acrophobia (with sometimes a compulsion to jump from said height), along with a fear of crashing (who does not have that fear?).

I believe I can blame my Uncle Doc for a certain amount of my phobia. He and my Aunt Alice, along with their two sons, Morris Jean and Mousey (the cousin I told you about with my daddy and the beehive), lived near Kilgore where Uncle Doc worked for an oil company, looking after some oil pumps. He owned a Cessna and flew to Cleburne to visit with us when I was about twelve. His arrival was rather spectacular since he buzzed low over our house on Sabine Street, getting everybody's attention, including the police. Please remember doing zany things sort of ran in my family, especially on the male side. The females were rather boring and rarely got in trouble.

Needless to say, when Uncle Doc landed at the airport west of town, he had a reception waiting for him—a number of us kinfolk and the police, who served him with a ticket. Uncle Doc just laughed; I do believe he was the most jovial uncle I had and was always smiling. He then offered to take some of us up in the plane if we wanted to. Usually, as you may have learned by now, I am fairly adventurous, but I was not too sure about going up high in that little bitty airplane. For some unknown reason, Uncle Doc looked at me and said, "Come on, Bullfrog. Give it a try."

Now if he had asked for volunteers, he would still be waiting for me to speak up; but now that he had selected me, I had to step up, right, guys? My male pride was on the line, and I manfully said, "Sure!"

Inside, I wasn't feeling so sure at all; but Uncle Doc and I crawled in, and he showed me how to buckle up. How does one know if he or she will have a queasy stomach on an airplane if you have never flown in one? I knew those flying swings at county fairs gave me trouble, as did the tilt-a whirl, but I did not know about this plane. I just knew I was not a happy camper, and Uncle Doc did not help once we got up in the air. He immediately yelled, "Hang on" and rolled the plane completely over, with me screaming all the way. Afterward, he aimed that thing straight up till the plane almost stalled and then plummeted downward until it seemed we were going to crash into the ground. That was all my poor stomach could take, and I plastered the floor of Uncle Doc's plane with what I had had for breakfast. He set the plane down pretty quickly, and I staggered off that thing, just about wanting to kiss the ground in thankfulness ala the pilgrims at Plymouth Rock. My sister Melba said you could just about count every freckle on my face; it was so white. Needless to say, that was not a pleasant introduction to the art of flying.

Believe it or not, I did not fly again until twenty-one years later in 1974 when my Granpa Reed (the one who nearly got in a fist-fight with Daddy at the baseball game) died in Carmi, Illinois; and I was going to attend the funeral. However, there were some complications. My wife, kids, and I had been down at Port Aransas for a week, staying in a cabin that her parents owned. Naturally, there was no phone, and this was long before cell phone days; so no one had been able to notify us until we arrived home Friday night, with Granpa's funeral scheduled for Saturday afternoon at two. I quickly called American Airlines at D-FW and scheduled a flight out at 9:00 a.m. the next morning. At the time, I had never flown on a passenger jet. Again, some apprehension set in, and what transpired the next morning did not help. We were living in Paradise in Wise County at the time, where I preached part time for the Church of Christ there, and we were about an hour and a half from D-FW airport.

I had set the alarm for six o'clock but slept through it until seven thirty, being so exhausted from the seven-hour drive the day before and not getting much sleep that night, thinking about losing Granpa. I did not have time to take a shower but just jumped into my clothes and headed east for D-FW. Fortunately, I had packed my suitcase the night before and just grabbed it on the run. Racing down Highway 114 at about a hundred miles an hour, I screeched into the parking lot at the airport and pulled an O. J. dashing through the terminal, looking for the right gate. I was the last passenger to board, barely in time, panting, sweating, and out of breath. To make matters worse, they placed me in a window seat. What was the problem with that, you might ask? Well, the week before, while sitting in my doctor's office, I had read this magazine article about a plane flight over New Mexico where a two-hundred-pound man had been sucked through a window! Now I am sitting by one, and at the time, I weighed about the same as the aforementioned gentleman. My apprehension had escalated somewhat to near panic.

This panic had increased to fright at take-off. No one had told me the horrendous noise and terrible vibration that occurs when the plane is blasting down the runway, trying to lift off. Man, I went through every prayer I had ever heard! After we leveled off, I relaxed a little, but the thought of that window blowing out and the grown man following it kept running through my mind. I then attempted something probably rather feeble in retrospect, but it was all I could think of to help my cause. I had my briefcase in my lap; remember I am a poor English teacher, and I am always having to grade no matter where I am going or doing (except driving myself). Thus, I had the brilliant thought to use my briefcase to block the window, which might save me from being sucked through it. (Well, it was better than nothing!) So I practiced a few times, ignoring the strange looks from the guy next to me.

The flight to Carmi was uneventful until we started descending and touched down. Again, no one told me about the loud noise, more vibration, and the teeth-jarring bounce when we hit the runway. And again, I went through a number of prayers, hoping to escape crashing. Fortunately, we landed safely, and my sister Melba was there to take me to the funeral for my final farewell to Granpa. We had seen him the year before when we had driven up to visit him and show him his one-year-old great-grandson, whom I had named after him, my second son, James (Jim) Reed.

The return flight home that night was a little more peaceful; but Monday morning, in one of my English classes at Fort Worth Christian College, something humorous occurred. In every class, it seems, there is one student who is a sage, a wise one with all the answers. I had recounted my rather traumatic tale of my flight to Illinois, and this student philosopher commented to me, "Mr. Reed, you had nothing to worry about. If it's your time to go, it's your time to go."

"Yes," I replied, "but what if it's the *pilot's* time to go? He gives me no option, no parachute! He just takes me with him!"

There's one in every crowd, right?

# CHAPTER 38

# MEMORABLE FUND RAISERS

How many of us have been backed into a corner where we had to "volunteer" to help with or even supervise a fundraiser of some kind? Well, count me in with that group. I remember three in particular throughout my life, each with unforgettable memories and certainly entertaining experiences for both those who participated (like me) and those who witnessed and died laughing in the process.

I've mentioned before that I once taught at Fort Worth Christian College, from 1967 to 1970. While there, the president of the college asked me to assist him with a fundraiser the school was hosting. Marques Haynes, the famous dribbler for the Harlem Globetrotters, was bringing another basketball team to perform, the Harlem Magicians; and the president wanted me to put together a men's faculty team to play them. I'm not too sure why he selected me to form a team; I suggested that our basketball coach would be a better choice. "Oh, he's going to play," the president replied, "but he doesn't have the time to find ten or so other players." I could see the challenge. Our junior college was a little small, and we only had about six men who would be able to move up and down the court. I thus did some recruiting at Fort Worth Christian High School adjacent to our campus. Three brave souls succumbed to my wheedling and cajoling, but that still left me one short. I wanted at least ten players total so that I could substitute five guys at a time. I had a preacher friend whom I knew was fairly athletic and would love to play. Charley jumped at the chance, and my team was set.

Since this event was strictly a fundraiser, I saw no sense to practice or anything. What good would that do? Our purpose was to serve as mere foils to Haynes' team anyway, so the more inept we appeared, the more laughs the crowd would give us. Game night came, and Fort Worth Christian's gym was pretty full, so at least some money would be raised for the school. We actually got to meet Marques Haynes after seeing him numerous times on television with the Globetrotters. Goose Tatum and Meadowlark Lemon served as the clowns for their team, but Haynes played the role for the Magicians, and he was good at it. He started off by borrowing the portable mike from the announcer and walking over to the scorer's table. He told the crowd that my team looked a little puny, so he would spot us some points. He proceeded to push the button until he had given us 40 points. I immediately told him, "Thank you. My team quits now. We win." Well, it was worth a try. At least it drew a little laugh from Haynes and the crowd.

The game commenced, although I do believe "farce" would be a more apt term. I'm trying to remember back that many years, and I don't believe we even nabbed one rebound—their center was seven feet tall. Charlie was our tallest player at 6'1". Naturally, they scored at will while our shots would get blocked, stolen, or missed. Meanwhile, Marques was performing as the court jester with his dribbling displays and behind-the-back passes. Plus, the way the other players would whip the ball around and down the court was sheer magic. In addition, Haynes pulled his fake throwing a bucket of water on the front-row crowd, who all ducked and screamed, but it was only filled with confetti. Then toward the end of the game (they're leading us by fifty points now) I'm dribbling the ball down court, and Haynes ran up behind me and grabbed me. The referee immediately blew his whistle and yelled, "You fouled that man!"

Haynes replied loudly, "I did not! I hugged him!"

Of course, that drew a big laugh from the crowd. Then I stepped to the free-throw line to score my only point or points of the night—a roar would go up from the crowd. Just as I started to release the ball from my hand toward the basket, Haynes leaned in and pulled the hairs on the back of my leg, causing me to miss the backboard entirely. This got a *big* laugh from the crowd.

The grand finale, of course, was Haynes' waving all five of my team to encircle him and try to take the ball away. Right! I'd seen professionals on TV try to do that and fail, but we tried mightily, just to keep the crowd laughing. It was truly a memorable night.

Another notable fundraiser occurred a couple of years later in the town of Paradise; I've mentioned earlier that I was preaching part time there for the Church of Christ. The parent-teachers group there was having a fundraiser for the school to aid with such things as textbooks or new lockers, whatever had been voted on that year. The event was going to be a donkey basketball game. At the time, I had never heard of such a thing, but I was asked if I wanted to partic-ipate as one of the players. They were needing ten brave (or stupid) souls who would ride donkeys while attempting to score baskets. I thought, "Well, how difficult can that be? The ball is still round, and the basket is still there. Let's do it." So I volunteered, not really knowing what I was letting myself in for. Now I was also serving as the high school football announcer play-by-play man, and my color announcer was Johnny, who also taught high school math. He and I were truly the Don Meredith and Howard Cosell of Parker County, and we definitely had fun in that booth. Johnny also signed up for the donkey basketball game, and he had played in several before. He assured me it was a lot of fun; he just didn't say that it was fun for the crowd but not necessarily the players.

The night arrived, the gym was packed, we players were instructed to line up at the backdoor and grab a donkey by its reins as they were unloaded from their trailer. I was first in line, eager to grab my gallant steed for the night, but the first "donkey" through the door was chest high to me! That thing was a *mule*, not a donkey. I just let him trot right on by, and I grabbed the next one, a much smaller one that I could just about step over. Yessir, that was the one for me. Unfortunately, my poor announcing buddy, Johnny, wound up with the mule, and I guarantee you that thing was a bucker. Johnny spent most of the night getting up off the floor. Meanwhile, the two captains, me for my team and another high school teacher for his team, rode our mounts to the center jump circle and attempted to catch the ball when the referee (the owner of the donkeys) tossed the ball up, and the game was on.

I grabbed the ball and kicked Mighty Mouse (my name for my donkey) in the ribs with my tennis shoes, and down the court he trotted. I'm looking ahead at the basket while my donkey was merrily trotting along. Suddenly, he stopped on a dime, dropped his head, and threw up his hindquarters, throwing me right over his front shoulders. Now the basketball and I were both bouncing down the court. Cue in here hilarious laughter from the crowd. I don't think many points were scored in the game. The entertainment, of course, was the challenge each player had trying to get his donkey to cooperate so somebody could make a basket.

Starting the second half, we were permitted to trade donkeys if anybody were willing. Poor Johnny, no one would agree to trade with him, but I found a poor sucker, I thought. I asked the other player did his donkey buck; he said no, and I assured him mine didn't either. That was good enough for both of us, and off we went, confident the second half would be different from the first half. Someone tossed me the ball, and my new companion and I were off to, again, score my first points of the game. Sure enough, this donkey was trotting right toward the basket and wasn't stopping on a dime in an attempt to throw me over his head. We were getting closer, about fifteen to twenty feet away, and he's not bucking either. Now we were approaching the basket from the side, and I pulled back on the reins to stop him for an easy shot, but he didn't stop! That was his trained trick—once he got close to the basket, he would pick up a little speed and never stop. Oh, well, at least I wasn't still having to pick myself up off the floor like someone else I knew.

A final fundraiser that still remains with me also occurred at Paradise. Every year at Halloween, the PTO (parent-teachers organization so they would not have to pay national dues to the PTA) would hold another fundraiser at the gym. Again, the funds garnered at the Halloween carnival would go solely to benefit the school. When I first moved there, I was asked if I wanted to volunteer to help in some way. The only thing that interested me was participating in the spook house. I wanted to scare the dickens out of those kids, and I knew how to do it. We held the spook house in the junior high football locker room, complete with bathroom stalls. I would use one of those stalls for my lair. Lair, you might ask. Yes, for here is what I did every Halloween for the seven or eight years my family and I lived in Paradise. I would drive into Fort Worth to Harris Costumes over near Casa Manna and rent a full gorilla suit. If I remember correctly, it cost thirty to forty dollars, but it was always worth it for the entertainment it gave me. One of the ladies working the spook house would lead a small group of kids into the dimly lit locker room, having them feel eyeballs (peeled grapes), red slimy intestines (spaghetti), and various dead animal skulls. When she had finished her spiel, I would then jump out of the nearby bathroom stall, dressed in the gorilla suit and growling as ferociously as I could. Naturally, those kids would be bouncing off each other, trying to get out that door. Sometimes for an added effect, I would chase the last little boy or girl back into the gym and around the room with parents laughing away.

One year, I added a special effect. In September, my father-in-law had deer hunted in Colorado on an early trophy hunt and brought back a carcass for me. I cut all of the meat off it, packaged it, and put the meat in a frozen locker that I had rented at the icehouse in Bridgeport. I also kept the rib cage, after trimming nearly all of the meat off it and saving that for chili. I had a plan for the rib cage come Halloween. Yes, this time, when I was hiding in the bathroom stall and jumped out, I growled and grunted while waving the rib cage in the air.

Now I wonder why those kids absolutely disappeared in no time flat.

# CHAPTER 39

## EATING CROW PIE

Surely most of us, from time to time, have been called upon to "eat crow pie." Wikipedia defines this as "humiliation by admitting having been proven wrong after taking a strong position." Yes, that pretty well describes an event that occurred many moons ago, about forty years or so, but the experience is still just as vivid now as when it happened. And, yes, I still cringe even thinking about it.

Any other relics of male chauvinism like me still remember the name Bobby Riggs? Well, I do, much to my chagrin and shame. Riggs was a former world champion tennis player in the 1940s and 1950s; then he retired and played exhibitions, along with gambling profusely. In 1973, the two highest-ranking women players were thirty-year-old Margaret Court of Australia and twenty-nine year-old Billy Jean King of the United States. Riggs had the brilliant idea of challenging one of them to a tennis match to prove that women were no match for men on a tennis court, even against him, who was fifty-five years old at the time.

Riggs first challenged his fellow American, but King was not interested. Then he flung down the gauntlet to Court, and she accepted. The two met on Mother's Day, May 13, 1973, in California. Riggs gave her a bouquet of flowers in honor of the day, and she curt-sied in response. Then the debacle was on. Riggs absolutely destroyed her with lobs and drop shots, winning easily, 6-2, 6-1. It was called the Mother's Day Massacre. Other male chauvinists and I, naturally, were euphoric.

Now a hue and cry went up from females everywhere, tennis players and non-tennis players, for King to step forward and defend the honor of feminists throughout the world. This time, King accepted, and the battle lines were drawn. The debate raged ubiqui-tously and certainly at TCC—South Campus where I was teaching at the time. Of course, yours truly was leading the dispute on behalf of our male population. I was discussing the upcoming match with two female friends of mine on campus: Martha, a sociology teacher, and Kathleen, a secretary. I was so confident that Riggs would win for, after all, I had seen his destruction of Margaret Court, and I knew that King would suffer the same fate. To be exact, I made a wager with the two ladies. I stated that if King actually had the luck to win, the two of them could paint a sign for me to wear, and I would dutifully wear it to my three classes on the Friday after the match (it was held on a Thursday night).

The epic battle was called The Battle of the Sexes, and it took place in the Houston Astrodome on September 20, 1973. Oh, well, do I have to continue? This time, King destroyed Riggs, 6-4, 6-3,

6-3. This time, Riggs played like a fifty-five-year-old, clearly over-matched, so was I in my boastful wager. However, I manfully showed up at my office the next morning on campus. Eureka! The two ladies were not there. Maybe they had forgotten the wager! No such luck. I ambled over to Kathleen's office, and there, my fate awaited me. Martha and Kathleen did not have just one sign for me to wear—they had two! They tied them on me, front and back, like the old sandwich man, a human billboard. The signs contained such statements as "The Pig Is Dead!" "The Mouth Is Shut!" "Long Live the King!" Oh, woe is me! However, a bet is a bet. I was ready to eat my words, so to speak.

Now Martha was very sweet about it; she was content for me to just wear them across campus to my three classes. However, Kathleen was merciless. She led me by the arm through the Student Union Building, amidst much laughter, I might add. In addition, then she led me through the library and the faculty wings. She finished the tour by stopping by the Collegian, the campus newspaper office, yes, where pictures were taken for the next publication in one week. Ouch!

Crow pie is not too difficult to eat if you chew fast and swallow quick.

# CHAPTER 40

## TUPID BIRD AND KINK THE CAT

All of us have owned some distinctive pets from time to time, and I'm no different from anyone else. Reaching back into recollection's vault, I remember the only bird I owned except for injured ones that I encountered from time to time as a young boy and tried unsuccessfully to nurse back to health.

This bird I'm speaking of was a light-blue parakeet that my wife and I bought in 1963 when we were living in Haltom City. She and I had just completed our Bachelor's degrees, and she had been hired by the Birdville Independent School District to teach first grade at Browning Heights Elementary on Nadine Street off Stanley-Keller Road. We purchased a house on Nadine three blocks from her school while I commuted to North Texas at Denton to complete my Master's degree. We still had our Bebe dog at the time, but my mother-in-law had a canary, so the wife brought home this pretty little bird. For some odd reason (imagine me doing something odd), I chose to name the bird Stupid. However, our daughter Cindy, who was four at the time, was missing her front two teeth and had difficulty pronouncing the letter "s." Thus, she called the bird Tupid, and the name stuck.

We first bought a large gold canary cage, about four feet high from the floor up, and various types of bird seed feeders that you either attached to the side of the cage or hung from the top. Then I read several articles about training parakeets because I had never owned one. I first trained Tupid to sit on my finger by tying a light piece of fishing line about eight inches long on one of his feet and tied the other end to my right index finger. This taught him to stay on my finger, for when he tried to fly away, he would wind up dangling upside down beneath my finger. He was a fast learner, but that was only the beginning to what he did on his own.

From time to time during the day, we would let him out of his cage and let him have the run of the house. His cage was in the kitchen, which was adjacent to the dining room, and we would close off the bedroom doors but leave my study door open. Thus, I would be sitting at my desk grading papers, and here he would come zooming in and land on my shoulder or the desk. Sometimes, he would attempt to land on my head, but I had a burr haircut then, and he would just skid right off. Plus, I taught him to wolf whistle and pick my front teeth.

My favorite thing that he would do was autograph my students' themes. If I were to hold a student's paper up rigidly in both hands, he would land on the top edge and start merrily pecking his way across the top, leaving little torn spots all the way. I would forewarn my students about this when I returned the graded papers, telling them that my bird had autographed their papers, a mark of distinction, I thought. I also cautioned them that Tupid might have inscribed their papers in another way. If they discovered a green or brown stain down the back or front of their paper, my bird had lent a distinctive touch to their themes. The boys would laugh, and the girls would scream. That's funny. My wife and daughter would do the same when they found something similar in their hair.

Another antic of his would be to try and eat the end of my blue ballpoint pen. I would be taking notes on a legal pad or underlining major passages in a book, and here would fly in Tupid and land on my desk. Then he would follow along with my pen point, trying to eat it, evidently, or kill it at least. He would peck away at it, turning his tongue entirely blue in the process.

We lived happily that way for a couple of years until catastrophe struck. For some reason, my wife insisted on getting a cat. Now I had been a cat lover since I was three, but I immediately pointed out to her that birds and cats don't mix. Of course, she was adamant in her desire, so we purchased a Siamese. (Now to all you husbands out there, please note that I am the head of my household; but my wife is the neck, and she turns the head any way that she wants it to go!)

We named the cat Kink because she had a kink at the very tip of her tail. Naturally, I loved that cat, but we had to make some changes to accommodate the two natural enemies. Anytime we would give Tupid the run of the house, we would put Kink in the bathroom where her cat box was and close the door. Since the canary cage was so sturdy, we felt fairly certain that Tupid and Kink could coexist as long as the bird was safely ensconced in it, although Kink would sit beneath the cage from time to time, staring hungrily at the bird.

We *thought* the cage was sturdy enough. One night, we went to the theater. Upon returning, we found the cage knocked over. My wife and two kids began screaming, but I pointed out to them that there were no feathers anywhere. A cat does not eat the entire bird and every single feather. I said, "Let's search everywhere." Sure enough, I found Tupid cowering under our bed in the master bedroom, the farthest point from the kitchen. I carefully picked it up, and the poor bird was trembling all over. My vet had an emergency number, and I called him at 10:30 p.m. on a Friday night. Would you believe he asked me to meet him at his office in thirty minutes? He examined the bird and stated that he was in shock; it was up to the bird if he could come out of it. Well, in the morning, I was the first up; and poor Tupid was lying on the floor of his cage with his feet sticking up in the air—not a good sign. A very solemn funeral service then followed in a corner of our backyard.

Kink the cat? No, I did not shoot the blame thing; it was only doing what was natural to a cat. I secretly blamed the wife; I also blamed myself for I knew better. Kink seemed to sense that she could be living on borrowed time for she really tried to impress me, jumping up in my lap and curling up when I was in my easy chair or sitting at my desk grading. However, she also became a constructive critic of mine. She demonstrated to me that she did not like for me to read Old English aloud. How was I to know that she had such selective hearing tastes? I was now working on my doctorate at TCU and was presently enrolled in a class studying *Beowulf*, the Old English epic poem. We would be called upon from time to time to read passages aloud to the teacher and class. Naturally, that required practice, which I began doing at home. So off I started, "Beowulf mathelode, bearn Ecgtheow: Hwaet, thu worn fela, wine min Unferth."

Suddenly, I heard Kink coming down the hall. "Meow, meow." She trotted into my study and sat at my feet, continually meowing, and then she jumped up on my upper leg, holding on desperately and still meowing. Something told me she had an objection to my reading *Beowulf*, so I plucked her off my hip, set her out in the hall, and closed the door. Then I continued reading, but as I was doing so, I saw a white paw protruding underneath the door, clawing away, trying to get in. Another time she indicated the same distaste for my singing. On Wednesday nights, some of the non-song leaders at our church were asked to come forward and lead a song. My being only average at best, I practiced at home from time to time, but when Kink again leapt up my leg, I always kept the door closed thereafter. I didn't need an extra critic; the wife was enough.

We had that cat for nineteen years. She was special and precious, but I still miss Tupid.

# ABOUT THE AUTHOR

Reed is a retired college English teacher, having acquired his Bachelor's degree in English, his Master's degree, and completed three years residency toward his doctorate at TCU. He taught for fifty-four years at the University of North Texas, Texas Christian University, Fort Worth Christian College, Tarrant County College, and Hill College. He is presently teaching part time at TCC and Hill.

Growing up in Cleburne, Texas, in the 1940s and 1950s, Reed experienced a number of unique childhood episodes, some humorous, some frightening, all memorable. Hasn't everyone eaten rooster's eggs in order to fly like a rooster or witnessed a friend bite off a grasshopper's head or pulled snakes out from under rocks in a river or nearly witnessed a fistfight between your father and grandfather over a baseball game? Reed is not ashamed to admit that writing is a challenge, a chore, actually, but that enables him to empathize with his students.

In addition to teaching composition and literature classes, he also team taught a wilderness course where he and geology teachers took students backpacking to such places as the Grand Canyon in Arizona, the Gran Tetons in Wyoming, the Smoky Mountains in North Carolina, the Sierra Nevadas in California, and Big Bend National Park in Texas. Read inside to learn more.